ANCHOR BOOKS

THE HUMAN KIND

First published in Great Britain in 1994 by
ANCHOR BOOKS
1-2 Wainman Road, Woodston,
Peterborough, PE2 7BU

Foreword

Anchor Books is a small press, established in 1992, with the aim of promoting readable poetry to as wide an audience as possible.

We hope to establish an outlet for writers of poetry who may have struggled to see their work in print.

Following our request in the National Press, we were overwhelmed by the response. The poems presented here have been selected from many entries. Editing proved to be a difficult and daunting task and as the Editor, the final selection was mine.

The poems chosen represent a cross-section of styles and content. They have been sent from all over the country, written by young and old alike, united in the passion for writing poetry.

I trust this selection will delight and please the authors and all those who enjoy reading poetry.

Michelle Abbott
Editor

CONTENTS

To Love, And To Cherish	Shirley Frances Winskill	1
The Verdict	M W Lees	1
Wishing For An Angel	John Gaerty	2
A Secret	Helen J Cox	2
Life's Quirks!	R A White	3
New Horizons	W Lawrence	3
A Change Of Style	James Stubley	4
About What Being Over Fifty Means To Me	A B Chabaluk	5
Half Way Through	Rebekah Barlow	6
50+	Ruth Slater	7
Change Of Life	Molly Smithson	8
Proud To Be Fifty Something	F Foord	9
Me Dad	Jean M Senior	10
Entry To Heaven	Nola B Small	11
Born To Dance	Joyce M Hefti-Whitney	12
Time	Margaret Dennison	13
Love And Beauty	C H Nicholls	14
I Am The Cross	Barbara Cunliffe	15
Jesus	Patience Guerdon	15
Cross Words	Charlie Keenan	16
Untitled	Peggy Evans	17
Easter Vigil	Louise Swanston	18
Had You Lived Then (An Easter Poem)	Francis J Weavers	19
All Letters Answered	Philip Simpson	20
Top Of The Milk	Susan Skye	21
The Birthday	Shirley Read	21
Life	Christopher Rigby	22
Softly Through The Twilight	David Hall	22
With Homage To Noel Coward - Miss Worthington	Betty Barber	23
Untitled	D V Howard	24
Dear God	G Woodcock	24
Baby Mine	Edith Matthews	25

Winter Wonderland	Margaret Paterson	26
The Malevolent Space-Filler	P M Holloway	27
Untitled	Jean Smith	28
Do You Believe There Is A God?	May Cryne	28
Thoughts On Eternity	George Charnley	29
The Book	Dorothy Cornwell	30
Clinging As The Ivy	Eleanor C Goad	30
Untitled	M S Ball	31
Life	Sue Johnson	32
The Year Of Forty-Five	Sarira Tilford	33
The Gospel	Freda Flo	33
Lady's Companion	Ellen White	35
Let Me Lean Upon You Lord	J M Collinson	35
God Alone Comforts	Jennie Schofield	36
Farmworker	E Swann	37
The Cross And You	Irene W Dulson	38
50 Something	Margaret McGurk	39
Proud To Be Fifty Something	L P Bennett	40
Reputations	Richard Stewart	40
The Fifties	Alan Johnston	41
Half A Century	Maggie Roberts	42
A Woman's Work Is Never Done	M Beech	43
Half Century	Beryl Jones	44
Fifty Plus	Mary Seddon	45
Remember	B Casey	46
Untitled	Ann Osborne	46
Where?	Gloria Manning	47
Jonah's Prayer	Janet Llewellyn	48
World	C Bennett	48
A Fair Land	Peter Skye	49
Nearly Sixty	Ethel Williams	51
Waiting It Out In The Gulf	Sarah Doyle	51
Untitled	G Flower	52
A Portrait Of My Saviour	Jean Parkey	53
Conflict	Terence Hutchins	54
Burial In Bosnia	C Howlett	55

A Sonnet On The Death Of Young James	Robert Neill	55
Deep Within Love's Spirit	Paul Hutton	56
The Enemy	Carole Bloor	56
Imagine If . . .	Maureen Cripps	57
A Dark Night	Pat Brissenden	57
What Is A Friend?	Peggy Carpenter	58
What A Joy!	June R Pooley	58
Casting My Care	Pauline Hamilton	59
Jesus Is My Friend	Mark A Wright	60
A Cameo Of Easter	Daphne Brooke	61
Two Score	David Bridgewater	62
Seek The Lord And His Strength	Pat Dunn	63
People	Sheila Stead	64
The Key To Happiness	Anne Dalton	65
Instant Answer	Jan A Krupa	65
Our Eastbourne Holiday	Joyce Hacking	66
A Prayer	Peter Langford	67
Sea With Elaine	John Stevenson	68
Spreading My Wings	Maura T Bye	69
The Last Word	Nigel Courtman	69
Downy Dreams	Eric Davies	70
Pawn In The Game	Ian Towers	71
Easter	Marjorie Williams	72
How Sad	Liz Dicken	73
Caverns Of Contentment	Bernard W Grace	73
Appointment With Love	Heather Hennings	74
The Wasteland	Jan Ferrier	75
Me	Lyn Crossley	75
Celestial Blossoms	Margaret Paterson	76
Living Drama	Catherine Roberts	77
Caught And Locked	Jessica R M Cowley	77
Release	Elizabeth Whitehead	78
Quick Silver	Catherine Nair	79
I Communicate	Iris Bew	79
Oasis	Cameron Montrose	80
Untitled	Sarah E Beston	80

AA	Angela Howard	81
Resurrection	Briony V Lill	81
Lord	Josephine Blyth	82
Young Man From Jerusalem	Colin Newton	83
Easter	Morwen Pippen	84
Sucker	Lynda Huckell	84
To My Brother	Barbara Samson	84
Easter	John Elias	85
Queen Of The Cottage	Cheryl May	86
Quality Of Care	Grace Leeder-Jackson	87
The Poet	Paul Nicklin	88
The Lonesome	Anita Watts	89
Words Of Confusion	Carl Davies	89
Christianity	Peter Buss	90
Untitled	Millie Edwards	91
Timor Mortis Conturbat Me	D E Metcalfe	91
Becalmed	Joseph O'Shea	91
40 Wonderful Years	Barbara Holme	92
Soul Sung Blues	Charles Murphy	93
Healing Light	Marilyn Brierley	94
I Could Have	Muriel Rodgers	94
Money-Go-Round	Dave Arnold	95
We Of All Seasons	Colin Needham	95
The First Time I Jumped	Aaron Lee Vallance	96
Pleasure	Sheila M Dell	97
The Cross Of The Servant King	Patricia Griffin	98
A Nomadic Mind	T J Sewell	99
Sitting In The Past	Mac	100
Who Indeed?	P E Pinniger	101
. . . For Oonagh	Quentin de la Bedoyere	101
The Plan	E Julia Horton	102
Innocent	Desmond O'Donnell	103
God's Beauty	Sheila Winson	104
If Only . . .	S A Richards	105
Blank Canvas	Jan Noble	106
Autumn Leaves	David Edwards	107
Ann's Story	Ann Higgins	108

Searching	Sue Harman	109
Evil Or Good	Hammy	110
The Two Strangers	David Owsianka	110
The Globetrotter	Hazel Spire	111
Florence	Carole Wood	111
For God So Loved	John Jamblyn	112
My Life Is Like A Candle	Sandra Heffernan	113
Resurrection Ballads	Helen Shackleton	114
The Last Day Of April	Neil Tuffnell	116
Jesus Forsaken By God	Ethel Elizabeth Deeks	117
Easter Thoughts	Jacqueline Dunlop	118
When Alice Came To Stay	Elsie M Rogers	118
My Nightmare And Prayer	Kathleen Rose	119
The File	June Barber	120
Giving Up Smoking	Gisela Cooper	120
Redundant	F Jolly	121
Light In Them Eyes	W A Hodgson	122
Why	Dorothy Bassett	123
Five Days And Nights Of Hell	Claude Austin Lilley	123
Memories Of Youth	B D Daniel	124
A Moving Experience	William F Beck	125
Aurora	R G Head	126
Untitled	David Zita	126
Slave To Love	J Gayle	127
The Human Mind	Sarah Maycock	128
Your Castle In The Air	George Ponting	128
Holy Week	Delroy Oberg	129
Day's End	Vera Hardwidge	130
Easter In Abermaw	Sue Warren Richards	131
The Other Carpenter	Ron Clarke	131
Bushfire In The Blue Mountains	M L Mattay	132
Heart	Peter A Kelland	133
When It's Over	Andy Botterill	134
The Appointment	Karin Ailsa Robb	135
Trees Of Life	Erica Donaldson	136
PC	Joyce Pompei	136
Untitled	G Collier	137

Love	H Philp	137
To The Wimborne Bowlers	R Forbes-Jones	138
Home	V Lingard	139
Tansy	F Laing	140
Prison Contemplation	David Southall	140
Untitled	Stewart Larkin	141
My Heart's True Rest	Tristram Rae Smith	142
Summer Train Journey	Kelvin Barry	144
Postcode Slip-Up!	Laura Corti	144
Untitled	Margaret Williams	145
Renewal	W G Holloway	146
School Holidays	Dorothy Lane	146
As Once They Worked The Land	Jim Wilson	147
The Pioneer Of The Street	Marion Laycock	148
Life's Pleasant Change	Maureen Pettet	149
Making The Transition Without Tears	Pat Sleath	150
Solitude	S V Smy	151
Proud To Be Fifty Something	Nancy Owen	152
Happy Retirement	U E Kopf	153

TO LOVE, AND TO CHERISH

You love me like the misty rain that softly floods the stream,
   You cherish me to tenderness forever,
You say you will be there for me 'til lovers cease to dream,
   You set me as a seal no force can sever.

I touch your hand in passing, and no one else suspects
   the warmth that touch awakens in my heart,
My love is like the sunshine that a quiet lake reflects,
   But then, you've known this from the very start.

When first you placed upon my hand that sacred band of gold
   Our love was bound together throughout life,
For you were sent to me, my love, to have and then to hold,
   From this day forward I became your Wife.

Although 'twas many years ago, yet still our love is new,
   When last we kissed it was the sweetest ever,
I know you will be there for me until my life is through,
And, should God wish it so, - until Forever.

Shirley Frances Winskill

THE VERDICT

'Oh, you're fine', the doctor tells me - but I wonder more and more
Why the walk up to the bus stop takes much longer than before;
Why the steps up to the station are much steeper every day,
So I have to pause and get my breath to carry on my way.

But I like to see the postman when he brings a newsy letter,
(I just wish my arms were longer so that I could read it better);
And I like to see my nephews, for I love them very dearly,
And could join in conversation if they'd only speak more clearly.

Yet I openly admit disliking weather growing colder,
But I'm fine the doctor tells me - 'just maturing' - (growing older!)

M W Lees

WISHING FOR AN ANGEL
To Anna Scott a brilliant person and magic artist

She dreams an angel will be her lover
Awed by silver night's embroidered cloth
Longing to hold him like no other
He glides around in her every thought.

She dreams an angel will be her lover
A grand and handsome fellow in a crowd
Exploring the heavens under wingèd cover
Hand in hand while harps play loud.

She dreams an angel will be her lover
And they will live far above the clouds
A peace so rare they will discover
And the sun and moon will shine so proud.

She prays an angel will be her lover
Entranced by silver night's electric sky
Disenchanted with life's fake lovers
She feels, in her core, the urge to fly.

John Gaerty

A SECRET

I think I'll keep the secret,
the one about my age.
Thinking that one's life is like being
on the stage,
act all you want, no-one will know the truth,
my years are the secret, I've still got
my youth.
In a few years time I'll be an O.A.P.
but that is the *secret* between you and me.

Helen J Cox

2

LIFE'S QUIRKS!

Cold April - Spring abound,
Birds twittering - A new sound,
'How far away' you say, is summer
On the shore I see a plover!

Old people talk of summers past,
Our young faces look aghast!
They talk of balmy days and nights, -
We marvel and say - 'What a Sight'!

Perhaps we should dare to dream,
Then life wouldn't be - 'As Seen.'
Dreams of nuptials and divine nymphs;
These are those we'd like to glimpse!

New dawns herald fields of flowers,
For us all to pass many happy hours!
Forests seem to grow to massive heights;
Ponies stroll beneath - bathed in light.

For us this is the firmament;
As we stare up in wonderment, -
Careful - life will soon pass by,
Grab it now - don't let it away and fly!

Night eventually falls on our tiny world, -
Our life's banner all unfurled;
Trust in your God to guide your hand
Wear life to full - Like a Golden Band!

R A White

NEW HORIZONS

You're happy to have lived this long
You've whistled your tune and sung your song
You've handled shovels and wielded picks
You've pushed a pen and learned new tricks

3

Of course you might still hold the fort
but isn't life just all too short
New battles beckon, new vistas call
A new day dawns, new dreams enthral

With children ready to fly the coop
It's time to learn and not to stoop
The old life's evening's now High Noon
There's hedges to trim and roses to prune

What will you do with all this leisure?
Find new work or go for pleasure?
Study and swot for a college degree
or take up archaeology?

Or will you travel around the globe?
the lives of other folks to probe
Convert an ancient french abode or
find that sun before you're old

Whatever decision takes your fancy
Be like Reagan and keep your Nancy
for life is lonely on your own
with no one to nag and no one to moan

So fifty and over is for me
The time of life to do and to see
The wonders of the world abound
They only wait there to be found

W Lawrence

A CHANGE OF STYLE

The young ones say that I need glasses
That is not the case at all
The electric light is not so bright
And the print is much too small

Squinting over magazines,
With eyes' that cannot see
I'm fifty plus, but what's the fuss,
What will be,! will be.

People whisper nowadays
Their voices fade away.
I'm fifty dear, do speak clear!
That's what you'll hear me say.

With thinning hair, turning grey,
Combed back behind my ear.
Over fifty now, Take a 'Bow'
I'm just happy to be here.

A B Chabaluk

HALF WAY THROUGH

50 something
what a drag,
I feel like I've turned into
a right old hag !

My face so pale
it frightens me,
I now wear glasses
so I can see !

I like to pretend
the lines aren't there,
I try to look sideways
yet at me they still stare!

My highlights are done,
I've had them for years,
the grey, and the wrinkles
my two worst fears !

I brag as I say
'The kids keep me young'
but I wake the next morning
a blister on my tongue !

How did the years
fly by so fast?
and take with them
my youthful past

But never mind
to myself I say
I must make the most
of every day,

I must count my blessings
as through life I strive,
and be grateful that I
am healthy and wise.

Rebekah Barlow

50+

Where's my shoe?
I want a drink!
(Will I get my work done?)
GR-A-A-A-N - The cat's in the sink!

God, it's raining, yet again.
'Rachel - Come Here!'
We're not going to get to that playgroup on time.
That, is patently clear.

Lunch - then it's off to the office,
(It's more of a rest than home)
Work, but of a different kind.
I can be in one place - alone!

Away from the kids and chaos and cats!
Cheese and toast on the floor,
From being the sentry at the lounge door
Protecting the *art décor!*

Did I think I was going to retire?
Swimming, dancing was how I would fare?
Yes, until I had two little treasures, deposited - in my care!

To get my leisure and enjoy it.
I strive like hell!
I'll let you know what it's like - 50+
When I have the time to tell.

But blonde hair, blue eyes, a petulant smile,
Twirling around in style!
She's wearing her minnie mouse outfit
It makes my hard work, all worthwhile!

Ruth Slater

CHANGE OF LIFE

Living in retirement, determined to age -
What could suit the purpose better than the printed page?
Rumbling screeds to friends abroad had given joy, I hope,
Could that be a starter to maximise my scope?

I studied all the programmes, tracked the venues down,
Then joined 'Creative Writing' because it's held in town.
The class was so enormous we had to subdivide,
And which day of two options caused problems to decide.

The hopeful writers gathered showed some with expertise
And some who unconcernedly could barely cross their Ts.
Each week our classroom altered, we learned our way about,
We tried our best to understand what blank verse was about.

8

Our tutor gives us homework - though he insists it's not -
And when our work is finished, it's criticised a lot
By everyone in turn, with the final casting vote
Being given by himself on an outsize printed note.

Competition notices are handed to and fro -
But whether they'll be entered, I really do not know.
Experiences of others can help to broaden views,
But only time can beckon that so-elusive muse.

Certain of my classmates turned out polished verse
But my own poor efforts gradually seemed worse.
Platitudes and plagiarisms wash around my brain.
Will imagination never come my way again?

Molly Smithson

PROUD TO BE FIFTY SOMETHING

Well it's great to be over fifty,
At last life's going my way,
I'm proud to say I'm still quite nifty,
Things get better every day.

Now that I'm mature and worldly wise,
Well that's what I think anyway.
I survey the world with tolerant eyes,
Think I'll go for a swim today.

So much in life to keep on learning,
Each day something new to do.
Life is short and not for the burning,
Enjoy it, three cheers for you.

I swim and dance and watch my diet,
If I fancy a new dress
Well, what the hell! I go and buy it.
I spend money I confess.
Life's not for ever,
So let's enjoy it.
F Foord

9

ME DAD

Me Dad, he was a Yorkshire lad,
His life was hard, but not so bad;
He lived within a cottage small
On *Oxenhope Moor* 'longside a wall.
His Dad cut peat to make a fire,
for Wintertime was cold and dire.
When t'fire smoked and made a pother,
they'd clean up t'chimney - one way or t'other.
They'd take a bunch of heather twig,
a rope, a stone, (it must be big).
Then, t'chimney cleaning got agate
with heather on t'rope and stone as weight.
On t'roof went Dad - *His* Dad inside
(for heights his Dad could not abide).
Down t'chimney now t'contraption went,
to clear out t'soot was its intent.
And then with t'soot all swept away,
and t'fire re-lit at t'end of t'day,
With watter fetched from t'deep, cold well,
into a cauldron for a spell.
O'er t'fire to make it warm enough
to have a wash - for soot's black stuff!
When clean again and t'oil lamp lit,
it seemed like time to eat a bit.
Some oatcake, cheese and good, thick stew,
and so to truckle bed, and then, -
When t'cock crew - time for up again!
Aye, me Dad, he was a Yorkshire lad,
and I'm a Yorkshire lass me'sen.

Jean M Senior

ENTRY TO HEAVEN

Have you ever tried to
    contemplate
What will happen at
    the 'Pearly Gate?'
Will God be there as you
    enter the portals
Begging to exclude we
    mortals?
Will he ask, 'Ask you
    Muslim?'
And reply, 'No room for him.'
A Buddhist is the next in
    line.
The star of David is for
    Zion.
From Persia comes Bahullah's
    band.
'We can't have them!'
Will God demand?
Does all this nonsense
    recompense
Those who pray for
    penitence?
Each race and creed shall
    none divide
And God will welcome *all*
    inside!

Nola B Small

11

BORN TO DANCE!

For the princely sum of one and six, and if you got the chance,
you could enrol at Miss Reeds, do ballet, tap, learn to dance.
Her bulbous thighs covered in black fishnet tights, sprung into the air,
bright red sash around her thick waist, she discarded with panache,
                                                                    flair.
Her bunions almost burst from her shoes as she 'Arobesqued' with
                                                                    ease,
'Come along children, ' she implored, 'Fairies not elephants,
                                                              please!'
She wore theatrical makeup on and off stage, her ruby red lips a
                                                                  gash,
huge gold hoops through large masculine ears, tinkled like a gypsy,
false eyelashes like two dead spiders, a beribboned wig to match
                                                              her sash,
'Pirouette Girls, pirouette, with feeling', we spun 'Til we were tipsy!
Her contralto voice boomed relentlessly without pity or remorse,
we fought like cat and dog as to who'd be the panto horse!
Miss Reed was a trouper, a teacher of skill, with regimental
                                                            precision,
'No Mavis you will be the rear of the horse, that's my final decision!'
'Aladdin' was a great success, we were 'stars' on the stage at the
                                                                'Grand'.
We danced and sang with all our hearts, the applause nearly got out
                                                                of hand!
Proud parents, grandparents, uncles, aunts, cheered with all their
                                                                  might,
Miss Reed dabbed her runny mascara, 'What a wonderful Night!'
Weary homeward bound, 'Stars' travelled in full makeup on the bus!
We'd all been given a little gift, a memento from 'Her' to us,
This night would stay in our memories, the smell of the greasepaint,
The roar of the crowd, before had no meaning, now I was heady,
                                                                  faint,
I was Moira Shearer in those famous red shoes, Oh! to have the
                                                                chance.

I'd ignore dads remarks about Miss Reed, she couldn't be a man?
Lots of women have hairs on their chests, I'll protect her if I can.
Anyway, she could be a gorilla for all I cared!
'Cos I was born to dance!

Joyce M Hefti-Whitney

TIME

Time trots with me through middle age.
We galloped when we were young.
I've always been in awe of it.
Its merits I've never sung.

I've used it, abused it, gambled and raced it.
Now we amble along just fine.
No matter what you do with it;
It is its waste that is the crime.

Worked hard; played hard.
Watched babies grow and go.
Rearing days; weeping widow time.
All behind me now.

Ah! Now there's my three score coming.
I see it wants to run.
I'll make it walk; work less hard.
More time having fun.

Solving mysteries of foreign lands.
In the sun all day.
Finding a likely partner, to dance the night away.

Unforgettable memories -
a book that has been read.
Happy in anticipation -
of all that lies ahead.

Margaret Dennison

LOVE AND BEAUTY

The lady gazed into her looking glass
That wife and mother now aged fifty four,
She felt so very saddened and depressed,
And shocked indeed by everything she saw.
The face she saw was looking old to her,
With straggly hair, grey now and growing thin;
She looked with horror at two thick black hairs
Which grew quite boldly straight from out her chin.
She noted well the crow's feet round her eyes,
Looked at her neck and never missed a flaw;
Her hips seemed to grow wider by the day,
Her tummy so much fatter than before;
The figure that she saw exposed to view
Showed ravages of time, one can't undo!

Her husband looking on, across the room
Saw his beloved wife's reflected face;
Two sparkling eyes so full of love and life,
A woman of rare beauty style and grace.
He knew he saw a treasure quite unique,
So smart and feminine in every way
Who seemed much more desirable to grow
As all the months and years did pass away;
He said 'My love if I could live again
The one quite certain thing that I would do
Is court you just as I did years ago
And with much less delay, I'd marry you.
Darling, of all the wives I ever see
There's none who're half as attractive as thee'!

C H Nicholls

14

I AM THE CROSS

I am the cross,
The witness of his sacrifice of perfect love.
These are the arms that held him high,
The son of God condemned to die.
I am the cross that bore his shame,
I am forgiveness in his name.
I am the centre of his story -
Jesus who lives in risen glory.
I am the sign, for all to see,
Of peace and love and victory.

Barbara Cunliffe

JESUS

The prophets foretold his birth, his death,
He came this to fulfill,
For his only purpose in life,
Was to do the Fathers will.

He was the son of God, but a man,
In him there was no sin,
He lives a pure and perfect life,
Our very souls to win.

He healed the sick and fed the hungry,
And how they flocked around,
Then they tried and convicted him,
Whom in no sin was found.

They stripped him and beat him
Placed a crown of thorns upon his head,
They spat and gambled for his clothes,
Then decided they wanted him dead.

All his friends had disappeared,
For their own lives' they feared,
Jesus' thoughts were still for others,
'This is your son and this your mother.'

15

'Take care of one another,'
They nailed him to a wooden cross,
Two criminals at his sides,
One mocked the other shamed accepted
The pardon he provides.

The devil thought at last he'd won,
When Jesus breathed his last,
But by the resurrection power,
He can forgive the past.

This Easter could be your 'New Start',
If to Jesus you give your heart.

Patience Guerdon

'CROSS' WORDS

A man from Mars came to our town
To learn our words and write them down.
He time-warped here at Easter time
And so caused me to pen this rhyme.

We heard the word - 'cross' - used time and again
And noted downs its meanings, with galactic pen.
By Easter day; was it all delusion?
That that one word caused such confusion?

I told him that our God was very cross;
Man's sin had caused great pain and loss.
Our Creator's plan had gone astray,
As Eve and Adam sought their own way.

God placed a cross where we'd gone wrong
'Cos we'd messed up creation's song.
There was a right way; but we had no tick,
Guess we considered ourselves very slick!

But God loved us so very much
His son he gave us, the gentle touch.
That we might live for evermore
And cancel out our wrongs so sore.

Jesus Our Saviour, crucified
On that cruel cross, midst man's deride,
Bore all our guilt and sin and shame
That we might each one claim his name.

Now Man of Mars, as you've crossed over
From outer space to our fields of clover;
So Christ has bridged that great divide
'Tween Earth and Heaven, let's join his side!

Charlie Keenan

UNTITLED

Jesus was nailed to the cross
When they hung him to die on a tree
He suffered for a world that is lost
But he died for a sinner like me

My heart it holds such sorrow
My tears they are flowing again
When I think what he went through
In agonising pain

When Jesus prayed in the garden
He felt so humble and weak
He asked Peter to watch
While he said a few words
But when he looked he found Peter asleep

My life I thought was planned by me
But I realise now, it could not be
For the breath I breathed was only lent
My time on Earth was shortly spent
The book of life has been read through
And now dear Lord I come to you

There were times I did not know thee
There were times I felt alone
There were things I would not talk about
Like the cross the spear and the thorn
Until the day you found me Lord
And washed me of my sin
And now I praise and worship you
My Saviour Lord and King

Peggy Evans

EASTER VIGIL

Shoehorned in tiny courtyard, all stand hushed,
foregathering in memory of him
who rose again to life as he had said,
though minds had not yet grasped the meaning dim.

The dancing flames lick round the spindly sticks,
and wind enthuses them with gusty chill.
This purifying fire is blessed once more,
and with it our proud minds, to do his will.

Christ, promise of our yesteryears, is signed
on pristine wax. Christ, dream of yesterday,
and morrow's memory, Christ glorified
is studded on Light's candle, O and A.

As Love's brave light moves through the darkened Church,
we chant our threefold thanks and take our own
to draw from his. 'Rejoice!', the cantor sings,
as in our hearts we gather round God's throne.

This night will leave us reconciled and saved,
as listening in standstill time we hear
God's message down the ages, and we know
this history is ours, as year by year

the Red Sea parts for us and stays its course,
and God makes trial of faith, yet sets us free;
walks on before us as a cloud, a fire,
and leads us to clear waters, till we be

full-cleansed, refreshed, and pure in heart and mind,
baptised anew, united with the blest,
confirmed, renewed in faith; communicants
in richest ways, our love of Christ confessed.

Louise Swanston

HAD YOU LIVED THEN (AN EASTER POEM)

If you have lived in Jesus' day,
And seem him smile and heard him pray,
And seen him make the blind to see,
Take little children on his knee.
O tell me friend where did you go,
As he for sinners suffered so?

If you had lived in Jesus' day,
Had heard him say I am the way,
Had seen him make the lame to walk,
The deaf to hear, the dumb to talk.
O tell me friend where did you stand,
As darkness covered all the land?

If you had lived in Jesus' hour,
Had seen him manifest his power,
As demons they obeyed his voice,
Causing Legion to rejoice,
O tell me friend what did you think
When he that bitter cup did drink?

What if near him you then did live,
Had heard him pray, 'Father forgive,
They know not that for them I die,
Then it is finished,' heard him cry,
Do you remember that he said,
I shall be raised up from the dead?

O tell my friend did your heart break,
As even God did him forsake,
As him they laid in borrowed grave,
The one who came this world to save?
O tell me all you saw and heard,
For I would cherish every word,
For I would know this love divine,
Given to us at Easter-time.

Francis J Weavers

ALL LETTERS ANSWERED

ALA, N(on) S(moker), lots of TLC,
Abbreviations come and go
In futile Personal Ads,
But in column after column
The fact remains the same;
For all the hapless Lonely Hearts
It's a sad, depressing game.

All Letters Answered, lots of
Tender Loving Care -
A simple, basic, common need;
A common, cold despair.

Philip Simpson

TOP OF THE MILK

Come into my warm abode
Please take a chair
Tell me what your problem is
Whilst you're sitting there
Clasp your hands in your lap
Feeling more secure
Let yourself be comforted
The story will pour
Out the sorrow, in the joy
Understand your pain
Nobody is perfect
And you are not vain.
People from all walks of life
Have suffered worse than you
Don't ever think that you're alone
That is not true.
Get things into perspective
Try to see the light
Talk it over with yourself
Don't give up the fight
Make a plan and keep to it
Sell yourself supreme
Have the strength and determination
Believe that you're the cream!

Susan Skye

THE BIRTHDAY

Five years ago today - a son - brother to Jane
The fourth side of the square
A full house
A family.

Five years ago today - a heatwave, burning pavements
Parched grasses, hay fever
No so much born as sneezed into life!

21

Five years - loving, tiring, tender, frustrating, absorbing
Broken nights, dawn choruses - outdoors and in!
Gurgling, crawling, toddling
The whole world to be explored.

Five - a baby no more, a boy too soon
Boundless energy, interminable questions
Experiment, rebellion
And now, schoolfriends to tea.

Shirley Read

LIFE

Life has no beginning and no end,
It is intractable and full of shadows,
From the moment you are born you are destined to die,
And then a new circuit of anguish takes place,
Unless you pass the gates of life and death and enter the garden
of infinite peace.
Life is a puzzle, every day is a new section.

Christopher Rigby (15)

SOFTLY THROUGH THE TWILIGHT

Now softly comes the glowing twilight,
A sigh that welcomes the end of the day,
Calm now the thoughts, that troubled the heart,
With comforting words a friend stopped to say.

Dreaming without sleep is the pastime now,
Memories a mixed blessing, with pain some you recall,
A gentle weathered face, holding a kindly smile,
Worn hands lie peaceful clutching a rag doll.

The last beams of sunlight reflect from a neighbour's window,
Rainbow colours clinging to the wall, afraid to let go;
Time was that every room shone with joy and laughter,
Happy families were played, till the lamps burnt low.

Now that so many yesterdays have passed,
When a nightingale's song through the dusk, showered the earth;
Like the scent of flowers, sweeping the night air,
The darkening skies would echo aloud, with its ringing mirth.

Grace is a gift that comes softly in the twilight,
Hopes for tomorrow still burn, but with less human fire;
Life's harvest is safely gathered in, and well stored,
This time, this place, and nothing left to desire.

David Hall

WITH HOMAGE TO NOEL COWARD - MISS WORTHINGTON

My mother, Mrs Worthington had always made it clear
That in the realm of theatre I would have a great career.
She said that my charisma would be bound to take me far
And I would end up one day as a famous showbiz star.
But Mr Noel Coward with this did not agree,
And told my mother bluntly that it wouldn't do for me.

'Don't put your daughter on the stage,' he gave as his advice
'Find her an occupation that is ladylike and nice.'
He said, 'The few good qualities she is lucky to possess,
Are not the kind of attributes to guarantee success.
And 'though she is undoubtedly impeccably well-bred,
For heaven's sake find something else for her to do instead.'

Alas, this well meant counsel my mother did not heed,
And packed me off to drama school with the utmost speed.
The teachers there did everything their knowledge to impart
Of the technicalities of the thespian art.
To walk on gracefully they said I had to master,
Not crash into the furniture and end up swathed in plaster.

Learn the lines and render them in clear and vibrant speech,
Not mumbled incoherently nor in a high-pitched screech.
Gielgud and Olivier and others I could name
Did well and went on later to join the hall of fame.
But after years of studying my progress there was slack,
'As far as acting goes' they said, 'you haven't got the knack.'

Betty Barber

UNTITLED

How much shall I remember
When I am tired and old?
What threads of recollection
Will gleam like threads of gold
Upon life's faded fabric
The fabric of the years
Time wears away the colours
The pattern disappears
The things that brought great sorrow
Glows faint and fades away
The hopes the disappointments
The dreams of yesterday
The trails that now I follow
May vanish in the blue,
But this will last forever
My memory of you.

D V Howard

DEAR GOD

Will you save me a seat in heaven
Make sure it's the one next to you
It's not that I'm greedy, sinful or needy
But if anyone needs it I do.

I'm not what you'd call a disciple
But please don't discount what I say
Just give me some proof, then Ill know it's the truth,
An answer would do when I pray.

It's hard on a day to day basis
When you've taken the ones we hold dear
To believe there's a place, where we'll meet face to face
And the reasons for all become clear

When it's my turn to climb up the stairway
Don't snub me or cast me aside
Remember this query, from someone quite weary
And pull up a chair by your side.

G Woodcock

BABY MINE

No sorrow for tomorrow baby mine for thee,
Only blue skies and sunshine and the sweetest smiles you will see,
The brilliance of my precious jewel this world can never dull,
For there among His angels you shine in heavenly love,
God could not watch one so pure and sweet get tarnished here
below,
So he took my precious jewel
In his own crown to glow, with happiness and contentment
This world could never know,
I know my precious jewel is safely in God's love,
He will, I know, give you my darling
All my fondest love.
Good night! God bless you!
Darling baby mine.

Edith Matthews

WINTER WONDERLAND

May we ever hope my love
To witness once again
Such a wondrous beauty
As we did that winter's afternoon
When we walked out to take the air,
It was a day spun with magic
Laid upon the earth by an unseen sorcerer
Like a jewelled cloak, frosted, splendent
The earth and air were as one
Clean and crisp and good,
I felt upon my weathered face
The warmth of a soft, soothing kiss
As laid upon the skin of a maiden fair
By the touch of a pale and wintry sun
Shyly making its first advances
From a far and distant cloud filled sky
Carried forward by an ever changing mood
While the very sky itself did seem
To carry us onwards within its spell,
The road before us sparkled and danced
Like a length of marcasite ribbon
Sprightly, floating free before our eyes
Blades of grass stood by the roadside
Silver dipped, encrusted in the last of snow
Seasoned with rough sea salt,
Trees stood tall and dark on the horizon
Extending long slim arthritic hands
Gnarled, cold and clawing hands
Wearily creaking their leafless boughs
Unstirred by the occasional gust blown
As a breathless wind swirled around us
Leading us further onwards towards
Our winter wonderland.

Margaret Paterson

THE MALEVOLENT SPACE-FILLER

See how quickly
  I devour this space
    See how soon
      I change its face

      Before I came
        You wouldn't look twice
        Now you're caught
          In Curiosity's vice

If you doubt me
  Look away!
    You need not read
      What I have to say

      You remain of course
        To the bitter end
          Reluctant to leave
            You new found friend

But I care for you not
  Nor any of your kind
    My purpose in life
      Is to waste your time

      If I don't get you here
      I'll catch you up soon
      In papers, in books
          Wherever there's room

The Malevolent Space-Filler!
  I get my way
    So now I will leave you
      To what's left of the day!

P M Holloway

UNTITLED

My dad lived in Yorkshire
I was miles away
I didn't see him often
Not each and every day
Then came the news that he'd been called
To Heaven up above.
I felt so full of hatred
For God I had no love.
I didn't want to speak to Him
I thought He'd done me wrong
I pushed him angrily away
He stayed with me so strong.
He said to me, 'My erring child
Just listen for a while
You think I took your dad from you'
Compassion was his smile.
'I only took him from the world,
Not from his loved ones in it
Whilst he's with me
And I'm with you
You have him every minute.'

Jean Smith

DO YOU BELIEVE THERE IS A GOD?

Some people have different ideas on this matter. My feelings are every person thinks about God. No matter what religion, colour or creed, they always seem to look up when talking about Him.

I will write about my idea of God.

Being brought up a Catholic, it is not always people of my religion who are good or pious. We have been taught, from infants, about God but so have most people. I have not always attended church, only on Sundays. But if anything goes wrong for me I think it is my own fault because I do not thank God enough for what He has already done for me, but I think He is there.

I know people who rely souly on God with their prayers to Him.
Some people do not pray at all but still think He is there.

I think of the tragedies, disasters but all are sent for a purpose. Look
at the wonders of the world, the earth, the flowers, everything that
grows seemingly from nothing. One hears of things that have
happened. Miracles.

If one lives up to the Christian faith one cannot go wrong. One day I
will know if there is a God and no longer 'just wonder'.

May Cryne

THOUGHTS ON ETERNITY

We need no Faith who must immortal be;
No darkness know, but light perpetually.
Eternal light no dark alleviates,
Wakes us anew with freshly cleanéd slates.
Time everlasting and space infinite
Doom us to life - no refuge give from light.
The darkness: sleep before each genesis;
We profit not from our insentient bliss,
For light is all we know - this is our fate;
In death we cannot differentiate.
Imprisoned in awareness always, we
Require no supernatural agency
To praise or blame for our eternal plight,
With darkness naught, and everything the light.

George Charnley

THE BOOK

There is a book which speaks of love
It's honest true and tender
To feel the comfort of God's love
Our hearts we must surrender
In our lives love must be found
We must be kind to all around
Free from anger and from pride
Let us in God's love abide
Against temptations he'll make us strong
Forgive the times when we go wrong
He'll strengthen our faith with special care
Proving his power through our prayer
God of goodness loving all
Please hear us when we make our call
If we seek we're sure to find
Our way to you brings peace of mind
We take knowledge from the book
Our lives become richer when we look
Through the pages of what God says
Giving to him our thanks and praise.

Dorothy Cornwell

CLINGING, AS THE IVY

Tenacious, as the ivy
As it clings to the trunk of the tree,
So tenacious is my love for you -
Is it so with your love for me? -
For the tree doesn't need the ivy
As the ivy needs the tree.

But, in time great trees grow feeble -
And sometimes, a strong bough breaks.
Should it be thus for either of us
As life its harsh toll takes -
Then, my clinging love will bind us
Together, for both our sakes.

Eleanor C Goad

UNTITLED

Books of hours
  and days
    and months
      and years.
Flowers
  and prayers
    and wounds
      and tears.
My soul doth magnify the Lord
  in golden scrolls,
    in canticles
      and psalms
        and outstretched palms
Down waves of winters,
  starved and frosted,
Burning summers,
  dried-out, dusty,
As it was in the beginning,
is now
and shall be.

In the beginning was the word,
and the word was good,
and the world was God
made flesh
  and bone
    and wood and sky and earth.

31

So we sang to the Lord with a joyful sound,
To the sky and the sea and the trees and the flowers,
To the sighs and the tears and the breeze and the showers,
To the laud and the glory and honour of all
    that the Lord had made.

And we lifted our eyes to the hills,
To the stars, to the spires, to the clouds, to the towers,
To the place from where the rainbows came,
And the rain and the snow and the wind and the waves,
And the help of the Lord,
  and the wealth of the world,
    and the healing of wounds,
        and the hearing of prayers,
          and the singing of praise,
            and the saying of grace.

To the graces of God,
  and the songs without words
    and the numberless times
      and the world without end
Through darkness and night
  to daybreak and light
    for ever and ay
      amen.

M S Ball

LIFE

What is it that we think about
In this life of ours?
Why are we so restless
And strangled by desires?
When will we be satisfied
And stop the strife for all?
Why does everybody
Always want to have a ball?

Life is wonderful
Life is grand
Think of all the happy things
That go hand in hand.

When will the desires of life
Come without a struggle and strife?
When will all the negative thoughts
Like rape and war and deceit and divorce,
All be taken over by
Multitudes of passers by?
And then perhaps life will be
All that is wished for by you and me.

Sue Johnson

THE YEAR OF FORTY-FIVE

Loneliness and fantasy,
        They stalked her middle-age
'Til secret loch and flying fell
        Her bitterness assuaged.

Beauty shared with dog and horse;
        This greater balm by far
Than empty words and doctor's couch,
        Or smoky, dim-lit bar.

Splendour of the glowing hills
        Melted the ice-flow heart,
And tranquil days her peace restored
        The best of life to start.

Sarira Tilford

THE GOSPEL

The Gospel's free to all mankind
It means 'good news' and life
No matter of what race or tongue
It brings relief from strife.

It is a record of God's son
Who lived and died for man
His words and works are written down
To show a well thought plan

To earth and as a babe Christ came
His birth was long foretold
He grew in stature and in grace
In wisdom manifold.

A lowly carpenter by trade
He moved among his friends
His twelve disciples always near
To learn and make amends.

With winning words he drew the crowds
The 'good news' travelled far
He lived a life of purity
No sinfulness could mar.

But there were those who envied him
Despised him and denied
And were not satisfied until
They had him crucified.

To man, this was the end of him
Until in three days' time
He conquered death and rose again
Triumphant and sublime.

He died and ever lives to prove
His love for you and me
And in return he only asks
Acceptance, personally.

'Good news' brings with it peace and joy
Forgiveness from our sins
Eternal life and heavenly love
New hearts from where hope springs.

How could we fail to trust in him
What better news be given
And I for one will worship him
Both now and in his heaven.

Two thousand years have passed away
The Gospel's still good news
Its message of salvation brought
To Gentiles and to Jews.

Freda Flo

LADY'S COMPANION

Stockings are falling down
Thin legs of ninety-three.
'This, is my gel,' you say.

'I was a model and proud,
But now this is my gel
To help with my dressing.'

Fur coats in Paris, once you wore;
And less.
But now, your hair-net's slipping.

Ellen White

LET ME LEAN UPON YOU LORD

Let me lean upon you Lord as you asked me to do,
Take all my cares and worries, I lift them up to you,
Your word says depend on you, giving you our trust,
To believe you will take care of me, my faith is a must.

Even when everything looks black, troubles do abound,
I will know you are very near, your love and comforting arms
wrap around,
If all my friends desert me I know you will be ever near,
Because you have promised your love and protection so I
need not fear.

So please help me to take heed and listen to what you say,
To be obedient to your word for this is the only way,
Let me lean on you Lord, take my hand, lead me for tomorrow
is a new day,
Let me hear your voice saying 'come follow me' for I know you
are the only way.

J M Collinson

GOD ALONE COMFORTS

When life seems so troubling,
Our emotions raw and bubbling,
Don't look towards another
For they are human too.
Often deeds are hurtful and
Words can sting like rain.
Thoughts turn in and boil
Causing turmoil and pain.
It is when these feelings surface
We just cannot cope alone,
Then we turn for certain comfort
To our God who leads us Home.
He is the only friend we have
Who understands our need.
He tells us - do not hurt inside -
Forgive the other's deed.
After all we are His children,
He created us as One.
He tells us - love each other,
Till life itself is done.

Jennie Schofield

FARMWORKER

Born to the land before World War Two
Grandfather Northampton bargee,
                              Father horseman
                              Uncles farmworkers,
All the family villagers through and through
                    I really love the land.
A childhood spent playing in lanes, fields,
                              by canals and streams;
Sunny days swimming, fishing, happy dog-days,
                              Robin Hood days,
                              ball-game days,
                              a champion in dreams.
                    How I adore the land.
School days over, the Seven Seas enticed me,
I even ferried troops to and from the Korean War.
Then a farm-trainee, agricultural student;
                              I found myself married
                              Tied cottage an' all!
                    I was back to my beloved land.
I ploughed amongst a snowstorm of seagulls,
watched the same old hare, run the same old run,
each night on my weary walk home.
Fed the stock, leaned on my fork
to watch them contentedly chew each cudding mouthful.
                    I relish every second on the land.
                              Until -
The years have blurred the horses into machines,
                              manure into chemicals
                              hand-work by sprays,
the gangs of men, women and children happily replaced by
automatons.
I lived on the land; lived off the land.
What a pity it's dying by man's greedy hand.

E Swann

THE CROSS AND YOU

Imagine yourself at the trial of Christ
Put yourself in His place that day.
After all His disciples had failed His request
In the garden to watch and pray.

He was feeling bereft after all had fled
His loneliness more hard to bear
As one He loved dearly betrayed with a kiss
And Peter the rock wasn't there!

All alone He carried that terrible Cross
We see Him walking with quiet grace,
The sorrow and anguish of His total loss
Showing in His beautiful face.

Picture yourself jostling on Calvary's Hill
With the mob on that bitter day
See Jesus, our Lord, as He accepts the Cross
Hearing you question Him - 'Why this way?'

Why this way, this suffering, cruel, savage way
For our Lord who came just to love
And save all the world from their sins and their woes,
To give Life everlasting above?

His eye seem to tell us with infinite pain that this
Was the only true way
That He could save us who trust in Him still
Till Faith reveals all on 'that day'.

On 'that day' when Christ once again shall arise
The dawn breaks and the shadows flee;
Those whose names are there in the Lamb's Book of Life
Shall share in His great Victory!

Today our Lord still looks down on the crowds,
He watches them choose the wrong way,
Let us not betray Him, let us make it known
He'll save all who will own His way.
Irene W Dulson

50 SOMETHING

Who would want to be like them
Old and done and round the bend
Life for them could not be fun
Life for me had just begun
My unsung song was to be sung

So up the ladder I began
I sat some tests and passed exams
My life was on the up
I had a great job and good friends
What more could anyone want?

Then one day upon my face a laughter line appeared
Oh no, what's this, how did that get there
Alas alak my eyes gave way and glasses had to be worn
'Twas then I discovered my laughter line had friends
Oh no, what has this ageing process done?

Then one day to my surprise
Early retirement did arise
I thought hard about this new role
To my surprise I had another goal
So out of the office I walked with pride
Lines and bags went side by side.

A new chapter has opened in my life
I never dreamt I was so up-tight
Now life's a pleasure and great delight
I thought my song was long past sung
But really life has just begun
Oh what will I do next?

... *it is not The End* ...

Margaret McGurk

PROUD TO BE FIFTY SOMETHING

I'm through the roaring forties,
I may not be so nifty,
But I am really doing fine
Now that I'm over fifty.

I'm not quite as energetic
As I was of yore,
It's only darts and snooker now
Not football any more.

Now that I'm a grandad
It makes me feel so good,
Those games with the youngsters,
Could be my second childhood.

So life begins at forty,
Yes, that's what folks say,
But now I'm more than fifty
It really is under way.

So this is my message
And I will shout it loud
For now I'm in my fifties
And I am really proud.

L P Bennett

REPUTATIONS

Never thought you had it in you
Said one of my English group
And I remember grinning with satisfaction:
It certainly did my reputation no harm.

A young boy he was, in Care,
Shunted round from home to home
A nuisance to most of our staff
A distraction to his fellow pupils.

40

Already some parents were muttering
Before that ill-chosen day he ran away
Across the playground, heading who knows where
To some dim hope he saw as freedom.

I was on duty, I called him back
Loudly with authority, most of the school watching
As he refused and kept on running
Until I sprinted after, brought him crashing

To the ground with a flying tackle:
Never thought you had it in you
He said, and his mates grinned agreeably.
It certainly did my reputation no harm.

Now I wonder, many years later,
What it did to that boy, to his esteem,
Judged in the eyes of the school a failure,
The boy who couldn't even run away.

Richard Stewart

THE FIFTIES

In pre-spect, half a century
Seems long in human terms
Retrospect, perspectively,
Brevity confirms:

Time's revalued,
Waste's eschewed,
Fools aren't suffered,
Life's renewed.

The joy of life intoxicates
And though the world may scorn
The fifties, it is not too late
To love. To be reborn.

To seize the day
Carpe Diem
Begin anew
To think once more, like youth

That life is full
And life's encharmed
Thirty years ahead
Seem forever
And they're better
Far
Than being dead.

Alan Johnston

HALF A CENTURY

I looked very hard in the mirror today, 'Good God who's that?'
        I heard myself say.
Your clothes are a mess - just look at that dress? They'd really
        give Oxfam a scare,
You're all lines and wrinkles, creases and crinkles, and birds
        could nest in that hair.
You're sliding downhill at a fair rate of knots, better slow down,
        ease on the brakes,
'Cos your face was never your fortune dear - and your figure
        isn't any great shakes.

'Go, soak in the bath for an hour (or two) it helps to get rid of the
        tension',
so it says in those books that deal with our looks (and problems
        too intimate to mention).
So I soak in the bath and now I've turned blue from the 'splash
        after bath with cold'.
Wrap up in a towel and hide from the skin that's saggy and baggy
        and old.

While still in my skin I step on the scales, then leap off with groans
     of despair,
The house rings with cursing, loud banshee like wails, with moaning
     and tearing of hair.
Go look for the book and the calorie chart and stop getting
     into a state,
One coffee last night with the last of the pie can't possibly
     add all that weight.

'Where's that miracle cream that promises each night to help
     me win this uphill fight?'
To banish the crows feet, the laugh-lines, the droop,
     a little used regularly, what the heck - use a scoop,
Pile it on thick and wait for the magic, now I look like a clown -
     whey faced and tragic.
Wipe it off, find the make-up, face paints and tints, the spray in a can
     that gives ones' hair glints.
There now - that's better, I look good as gold. So I should,
     it's my birthday.
I'm fifty years old.

Maggie Roberts

A WOMAN'S WORK IS NEVER DONE

A woman's work is never done
We sew, we cook, we clean
We dust and polish, scrub and sweep
No time to stand and dream.

We're on the go from dawn to dusk
No matter how we feel
We have to plan, we have to shop
And cook an evening meal.

The family comes home to tea
They buzz like busy bees
They shout together, talk at once
Why don't they ever cease!

43

Then off they go their separate ways
And leave the mess for you
To clear the table and wash up
With endless jobs to do.

Then all too soon, a quietness looms
The birds have flown the nest
The silence is unbearable
When you take that well earned rest.

You long for noise, and meals to get
And mess to clear away
The place just seems too tidy
Things in their places stay.

Then one day you get a call
Can we come home for tea?
Once more we cook and clean and dust.
For our family to see.

A woman's work is never done
I'm *very* pleased to say
We wouldn't change it for the world
Or any other way!

M Beech

HALF CENTURY

Can no longer stride up a hill
Often ache and need a pill.
Lots of flab and things hang down
Even though I walk to town.
Teeth are loose and hair is thin
And I have a double chin.
I need glasses now to see
Yet I think 'Oh dear me'.
How old my dearest friends have grown
While just me and me alone
Look unchanged by passing years!
Ignoring mirrors I've no fears.

Grandchildren running up the path
Oh to see and hear them laugh
Children grown and gone away
But they often come and say
Mum and Dad we love you so
So as the years so quickly go
We still have time to care and love
And thank our Father up above.

Beryl Jones

FIFTY PLUS

It's not a sin to be fifty, lucky you've got so far
Some folks think you're past it, you start to think you are
But that's when you start living, you look life in the face,
Seeing the mistakes you have made, in the half century race.

Now's the time to start making new plans every day
Time on your hands now, the kids are grown up and away
Plan a new hairstyle, a rendezvous for two,
Pleasant surprises for each other, just him an you.

It's lovely being fifty plus, there's lots of things to do
Adult education classes, keep fit and bingo too
Making new friends, and partners at the sequence dance.
Doing things you've wanted before, but never had the chance.

Grandchildren come to visit you, you hold them on your knee,
Reminding you of yesteryears, happy and carefree.
And as you say goodnight to them, your right to feel so proud,
Congratulate yourself, a job well done, a life so well endowed.

Mary Seddon

REMEMBER

Did you know that once I was just like you,
Rushing all day with so much to do.
Washing, cooking, cleaning all day
No fancy new gadgets to lighten our way.
With a houseful of kids no time to be ill
If only we had that joyous birth pill.
I had thick curly hair and sparkling eyes
And I'd look at my man with passionate sighs.
To my handsome young man I was his heart's delight
With strong loving arms that could hold him so tight.
But now that I look no longer like you
Sitting all day with nothing to do
But gentle with me with your kind loving care
Give a soft spoken word as you pass by my chair,
I know I'm a nuisance, I know I complain,
It's hard to keep smiling when your body's in pain.
So be kind and be gentle in all that you do
Remember my chair is just waiting for you.

B Casey

UNTITLED

Alright - I've passed 50,
No so nimble or nifty,
But not quite ready to fold,
The grey cells still jumping,
The iron keeps pumping,
As new interests replace the old.

Study skills I'm renewing.
Past events I'm reviewing,
I don't jog or climb mountains it's true,
But I'm full in my prime,
This is quality time,
I'm glad I'm past 50 - aren't you?

Ann Osborne

46

WHERE?

Where? said the donkey
        Am I being led
To an earthy, strawy manger bed?

Where? said the Virgin Mary
        Is my baby to be born?
She pondered in her heart words forsworn.

Where? puzzled Joseph
        Is this wonder to take place?
As he gazed at Mary's tender face.

Where? The startled Shepherds cry
        As the angels from them fly
Is this wondrous happening nigh?

Where? The wise men seeking go
        To find the King born below
Bearing gifts for One Divine.

Where? Joseph and Mary say
        Is that son of ours this day
They find him in the temple there.

Where? said Jesus, unafraid
        Why do you ask parents dear
About my father's business here.

Where? Mary remembered words
        Spoken of the babe she bore
Of the heavenly father's love.

Where? is he now
        Hearts have cried
Redeeming His world at His father's side.

Gloria Manning

JONAH'S PRAYER

The Lord my God is quick to save
He heard me from my watery grave.
Into the deep I was thrown
Engulfed in darkness, all alone.

In a flowing, swirling sea of death
The frigid waters took my breath.
Seaweed wrapped around my head
Caressed toward a miry bed.

I thought you'd turned away from me
When I was hurled into the sea
Yet as I was about to die
You Lord, in heaven heard my cry.

I lay entombed beneath the waves
Then you raised me from the grave.
My prayer had risen to your throne
For I was never once alone.

Those who do not worship you
Will find their idols false, untrue.
You alone have power to change
The 'natural' order, you arranged.

So I will sing you songs of praise
And give you thanks for all my days.
What I have promised, I will do
Because salvation comes from you.

Janet Llewellyn

WORLD

We live in a world where man no longer matters,
For now he has systems, his life is in tatters.
The conjuring tricks we apply to our lives,
Cause ample confusion, we fight to survive.

We live in a world where machines are abundant,
Their clinical action has made us redundant.
To maximise profit, firms try as they can
To update machines, whilst they minimise man.

We live in a world where people like speed.
But travelling quickly when there is no need,
Is to miss many sights that we may have admired.
Scenes that would have made artists inspired.

Religion's a matter which puts us to task.
It begs far more questions, than we dare to ask.
The answers we crave for are awkward to find.
To believe is like letting the blind lead the blind.

Governments feed us with falsehoods and lies.
On the media, pressure is subtly applied.
The stories we read in the everyday news.
Are disinformation and help to confuse.

Those men in control who manipulate others
Will soon be replaced by obsequious brothers.
Their creed will not matter, for once they're in power,
Their colour will pale and their sweetness will sour.

C Bennett

A FAIR LAND

Britain, the workers' demi-paradise,
Who keep their class distinctions
Seldom in disguise ...?

An island full of utmost beauty!
Where Socialists or Tories carry off their booty,
Whilst others are constant in their worries.

Britain! That mighty lion
That a century ago ruled the world,
Now, alas, in world affairs, has hardly any hold,
Except of course the BBC,
Whose voice still floats above the EEC.

Britain, the citadel of free speech,
Where everybody utters, be he poor or rich.
True, ancient Bodicea, here, failed her test,
But modern defenders - victorious -
Gave us peace and rest.

All is not perfect, nor was, or ever'll be:
Yet, when state after state fell,
Some through weakness, some through treachery,
She stood alone against the bloody tyranny.

How short is human memory ...!
So let me rephrase, put it another way:
There were other contributions,
And final push by USA,
But it's mainly due to Britain
That the West is free today.

Britain, a fair land by and definition,
To which many people have admission,
They come and go as they please,
For tolerance and fairness assure their ease.

Oh Britain! Your charm is almost haunting.
Here is the place to be
For all fair minded people -
You, you, you, and me.

Peter Skye

NEARLY SIXTY

What does being 50 plus mean to me.
Well let me think, now let me see.
I feel no different than I've always done
Sometimes I feel old, and sometimes young
I don't wish to change places with anyone else
In fact I prefer just being myself
My children have grown up, though one's still in the nest
But I have more time to do things I like best
I like reading and writing, and compose poetry
Tending my pot plants like Busy Lizzie
News and nature programmes I watch on the telly
Also Fred Dibnah, what a character is he.
I enter some competitions, and also prize crosswords
But I never win, I'm just given the bird.
My poems are printed in Charfield Newsletter
Now that I'm practised, I'm getting much better
All my friends like it, they think I'm quite good
They heap praise upon me, well of course friends should.
What do you think happened today, don't laugh
I signed my very first autograph.

Ethel Williams

WAITING IT OUT IN THE GULF

My heart it broke in silence
I thought that no-one cared
Each night I prayed to God above
That their young lives be spared.

My lad is one of many
In the burning heat they wait
Not knowing what will befall them
Or who will decide their fate.

51

I know there's wives and other mums
Who feel as I do now
All hoping for a peaceful way
Of settling it somehow.

One feels it's never ending
These battles to be won
My father, uncle, brother
And now it seems my son.

But I can't express the feeling
Or hold back the falling tear
For our brave lads so far away
We hold so very dear.

Sarah Doyle

UNTITLED

I miss you every hour of every day
And yet, dear one, I would not have you stay
If in the years ahead there would be pain
And maybe sorrow to be borne again.

I count my blessings as I call to mind
Our happy hours together, and I find
A bitter sweetness, in the lovely hours
That now are all my own, but once were ours.

I do the many tasks which once we shared
And treasure all the things, for which you cared
I conjure up your voice, and see your face
And thus, can be with you in every place.

My loneliness for you, that like a tide
Engulfs me now and then, I try to hide
Because I know with joy, one thing is true,
Each passing day is one day nearer you.

I only have to wait, and in my dreams
Relive our happy days, and if it seems
That days go slowly by, I shall not weep,
Since I have such a loving tryst to keep.

G Flower

A PORTRAIT OF MY SAVIOUR

No-one knows what you look like Lord, but you must have a
                                        beautiful face.
A face full of love and compassion, tenderness and grace.
How can I help but love you Lord, when I think of what you
                                        have done,
You died for me on Calvary, God's Precious Only Son.
You are the fairest of the fair, you are strong yet oh, so gentle,
Your voice is soft and tender, when you speak, you speak with love.
You don't have to say you love me, I can hear it in your voice,
I can see it in the tenderness of your eyes, those eyes so full of love,
With just the glimmer of a tear for the sin and sorrow here.
Oh, how I long to be with you, to gaze on your once thorn
                                        decked brow,
Your body for me bruised and broken, is full of glory now.
How can I describe a love so deep and true,
A love beyond human understanding, the love I feel for you,
And yet my love for you Dear Lord, is oh, so very weak,
When I think of your boundless love, that love that will never
                                        let me go,
That love that shines through the ages, oh Jesus make me love
                                        you more,
You I must worship and adore, you are the purest of the pure,
You shine like the sun, you radiate love wherever you are, you are
                                        the bright and morning star,
You are God's Beloved Son, yet you died for me, such a
                                        sinful one.
How can I show my love for you when I think of all you went through.
I see you there at Calvary, bearing the cross for such as me,
                            bearing its shame and misery.

53

I see your Sacred Head, drooping on your breast, the nails which
pierced your hands and feet,
The blood flowing, ever flowing for me, and I whisper your Name,
your Name so sweet.
You hung there on the cross, yet you uttered not a word,
Not a word of condemnation, though they crucified you Lord.

Would that I might be like you and turn the other cheek,
Show love instead of anger, oh Jesus, make me meek,
Make me meek and gentle Lord, that everyone will see
The love of Christ My Saviour, shining out through me.

Jean Parkey

CONFLICT

Bang goes a gun,
Bang goes a life,
There goes a widow
Who used to be a wife,
There goes an orphan
Who used to be a son,
Please dear, sweet God,
Something must be done.

Boom goes a bomb,
Down goes a home,
One of a couple
Goes off alone.
Blood on the pavement
Blood on his hands,
Heaven doesn't want him
Forsaken now he stands.

'Thou shalt not kill'
Our Lord hath said
They do not hear,
Those folk are dead.
Terence Hutchins

54

BURIAL IN BOSNIA

The boards are steady
Even the coffin's made ready
For the veiled and sombre mood
The mourners stand in
Not grinning a grin
But thinking of beer and food
Few are there
Someone combs her hair
While the vicar tries not to be rude.
The coffin is lowered
But many are soured
By the send-off he gets
It's so crude.

C Howlett

A SONNET ON THE DEATH OF YOUNG JAMES

Oh how horrendous is the thought that those
So young should do so cruel and act of crime
Taking a child in anguish through the rows
Of people who could help, but had no time.
Crying he went to meet an early grave
Shattered by rocks and heavy blocks of stone
His love of life - his smiling happy face,
Was this the sight from which hatred had grown?
Can we but guess what evils lay inside
Those two children - oh so young themselves.
How had the world instilled this evil side?
How much blame should we accept ourselves?
Was it the video nasties we accept
That spurred this crime, a crime we all regret?

Robert Neill

DEEP WITHIN LOVE'S SPIRIT

On a pleasant summer morning as they strolled along a path,
winding through the forest alone and free at last.
The birds were sweetly singing their joyful chorus spreads,
infecting into tender hearts the unyielding want of love.
Softly play the golden rays that flicker from above,
revealing all her splendour and unblemished features glow.
He stoops to choose a flower then decorates her mane,
with gentle fingers on her nape he guides her to his lips.
Pent up waves of passion burst forth in disarray,
searching for each other they swim in ecstasy.
Across the unknown threshold past pretence left behind,
the bond is sealed forever their journey is defined.
Deep within love's spirit there is a voice that calls,
demanding our attention to soothe an aching heart.
Deep within love's spirit there is a burning flame.
that shines for recognition, a light to lead us home.

Paul Hutton

THE ENEMY

Man is our enemy, this nature knows.
He plunders the seas, wherever he goes.
He is wiping us out, with no chance to roam,
This beautiful ocean, that we call our home.

Will man never learn, to give and not take,
Must he 'ere kill, for progress to make,
So someone out there, please heed our call,
Stop what you're doing, you're killing us all.

Carole Bloor

IMAGINE IF ...

Imagine if we could all be rich,
Life would go on without a hitch.
Imagine if we could walk on the sea,
A fantastic idea that would be.
Imagine if at the end of the day,
Everyone could get their own way.
Imagine if the blind could see!
What a wonderful idea that would be.
Imagine if a dog could talk,
He'd soon tell us, 'Let's go for a walk.'
Imagine if we could live for ever,
Never get old, but, get very clever.
Imagine if night could be day,
We would live our lives in a different way.
Imagine if we all had wings,
We could do such wonderful things.
Imagine if we didn't need sleep,
And be so happy we'd never weep.
Imagine if these things came true!
We might not be happy in all we do.
Rest assured, we'll imagine no more,
As life could get to be a bore.

Maureen Cripps

A DARK NIGHT

You walked away from me!
But glanced behind
A reassurance and acceptance.
I was so saddened.
It was as though You were walking
Along a concourse
To catch a plane
But I was not to come with You.

I must stand firm in my lonely skiff
Through whirlpool, buffeting storm,
Strong winds, through this dark night
Where the only sure anchor
Is faithful love.

Pat Brissenden

WHAT IS A FRIEND?

A friend is someone who can laugh with you, but can also laugh
                at you without giving offence.
Someone who can cry with you and cry for you when you are
                in trouble
Someone who is always there when needed, and can be relied on
                to understand.
Someone who - no matter how far away - can always say the
                right word at the right time.
Someone who listens when you want to talk, and only gives
                advice when it is asked for.
Someone who knows all your faults, and loves you just the same.
Someone like - *you!*

Peggy Carpenter

WHAT A JOY!

At Christmas-time a unique phase in history began,
Love from Heaven came down to Bethlehem;
In stable bare, a child was born in haste
To be a Saviour to the whole human race.
Oh, what a joy!

At Easter-time, a full grown man of thirty-three,
He was scourged, reviled and crucified on a tree:
Doom and gloom all around there was for sure,
'Til He rose again to live for evermore.
Oh, what a joy!

At Pentecost, His life-giving Spirit He did impart,
His power to inflame and dwell in human heart:
A comforter, sustainer, helper and friend He will be
To those who obey and trust Him implicitly.
Oh, what a joy!

June R Pooley

CASTING MY CARE

Lord, I see the fisherman, by the cool water's side
Casting his line to the middle where the river runs wide.
Hoping to feel that slight tug on his line
Waiting so patiently - he's got plenty of time.
He reels in the line and again casts it deep,
It lands where he wants it, where the fish now leap.
He knows his cast must be strong and firm,
There's no holding back this he has learned.

If I could be like the fisherman casting into the spray
I could cast all my cares on you Lord, each and every day.
But instead I hold on to them, and toss them around in my head,
They become a part of me, when I should give them to you, instead.
They become the burden I carry through life with me
Instead of nailing them to the cross, so that I can be free.
Lord, help me to cast all my cares upon you,
Help me to leave them there, then I can start anew.

What are these burdens we carry around,
They are rejection, disappointment and fears that abound.
There is violence and abuse and broken relationships too,
There is fear of the future, the past and anything new.
There are friends and family and all for whom we care.
Lord, the list is long, but I know you're aware,
Because you too have had cares in this world to bear.
You too have suffered, been weighed down, when no one cared.
And what did you do when your burdens were great?

You went to the hills and you stormed heaven's gate.
There you talked to your Father, and laid it all on Him,
Then you carried on with life, but with greater power within.
Lord, can I be that strong, can I be that bold and brave?
Can I cast my care on you, be a servant, not a slave?
Is it really possible to leave my burdens with you there,
Instead of carrying them around with me because I know you

really care.

As I read your word dear Lord, you make it very plain
'Cast your cares upon the Lord, and you He will sustain.'
So yes, I choose to leave my burdens at your side,
To leave them there, never to return, never more to hide.
I'll trust you with my burdens - so that I can now be free,
I'll trust you for my life Lord - we're together you and me,
And when the cares of life come on, as come on they must,
I'll cast them all on Jesus - the One in whom I trust.

Pauline Hamilton

JESUS IS MY FRIEND

Jesus is my friend
He's there when I awake
Each morning light
Jesus is my friend he's there in the darkest hour of every dawn
When I give him my thoughts
He traces the pages
He etches each passing cloud in my mind.
His golden light highlights my past,
Each special moment
Into the viewing machine that I can see.

The special years of football
Of running up that hill
Of freedom, the beautiful feeling
The tennis courts the dog dusty and my mother
Long summer evenings
Of playing just for Leeds
The white colour of innocence
Born to be infested by the dregs of experience
That encompasses time.
Each train ride
And cycle ride
First love, girlfriends
They sink into me like a sunset of clay
A form I can keep forever.

Like Richard my best friend
Of football kit Saturdays
Waiting on results
Or the Wimbledon fortnight within tennis balls blown . . .
In grass dust.

So Jesus is my friend when I look to the sky and ask why
And the beauty written in our foreheads
Is our character his thoughts
Wonderful burning gold memory
Atop the highland hill ...
So sleep little child
Inside your cube of rose scented childhood,
Even now!

Mark A Wright

A CAMEO OF EASTER

The frenzied crowd cry out against
　　The One who only helped the poor
And healed, and fed, and loved all men,
　　Spoke words of hope and comfort sure.

Our Lord, He wears a crown of thorns,
    They whip and jeer, shout 'Crucify'.
His heavy cross - our sins - He bears
    To Calvary where He must die.

The sun goes dark, and earthquake splits
    The rocks and graves. Fear fills the sky.
Creation groans in disbelief
    That God, who made the earth, should - die?

But no way else could we go free
Than Jesus dying - just for me.

As dawn's early light awakens the earth,
    A beautiful garden waits to reveal
Its secret sublime of joy for mankind!
    And flowers, trees and birds all burst into praise.
Come Mary and friends, with spices and balm,
    In love for their Lord - but what will they find?
The very large stone which sealed up the tomb
    Is rolled aside and an angel sits there!
'He is risen,' he says; 'He is not here'!
    Death could not hold Him, our great Lord of Life:
Love had defeated all powers of hell,
    Made a way back to God, a bridge into Heav'n.

From darkness to light, from death into life,
Come, kneel before Jesus, this Easter Day!

Daphne Brooke

TWO SCORE

A face looms towards you
And life reads another page
Fears run with the morning
Reflecting two score of age

The year waves goodbye
Scratching tales upon the dust
And life makes decisions
Your mind cannot trust

The mirror holds the evidence
Your years cannot turn
A glimpse of a memory
Your childhood does yearn

Your eyes see tomorrow
A shiver comes to pass
Hoping the cracks in the mirror
Belong to the glass

David Bridgewater

SEEK THE LORD AND HIS STRENGTH

A peaceful scene, a golden summer evening,
Dinner set out, the family gathered in.
The mother quietly pleased to set good fare before them.
Sat down herself, prepared to eat her food.

The times were stressful for her, and now and then
She had to fight her way through panic attacks,
Her husband always helping when he was at home.

But now the terror struck, suddenly, no time to seek his help
Or gather resources of her own.
She was falling, falling, into space. Or so it seemed.
Her very being, like two arms, stretched up, beseeching aid.
And was grasped by Another, familiar as herself and yet,
Completely Other. Drawn up by Mighty Power and gently
                                        placed in safety.
She was back, no time had passed, the family unaware.

Pat Dunn

PEOPLE

My sitting-room window faces the road and
I 'nick-name' the people passing by,
I'm not being nosy - just interested -
I really don't know why.
There is the 'Road Runner' who walks by
Several times a day - at the speed of 40 knots!
I think she's amazing and I admire her energy - lots!
Then little 'Andy Capp' comes by -
What a variety of hats I note,
And I much admire his well worn leather coat.
'Alfie Bass' shuffles along, he must have poorly feet
I'm tempted to ask him to rest upon our garden seat.
'Whistling Willie' the doggie walker, goes out in every weather,
So often looking tired and at the end of his tether.
The 'Old Boy' with his shopping bag, walking stick and pipe
Shops every day - sometimes with his wife.
The youngsters on their way to school,
Wearing bright, yet warm and sensible gear
Reminding me of days gone by, with just a little tear.
There goes 'Big-fella' and his jolly wife,
He's from the south and calls her his 'trouble and strife'!
I really must stop this and get a cup of tea,
I wonder what those people really think of me!
I'm sat here in my wheelchair, and unable to walk,
So, it would be nice if they'd pop in
And we could have a talk,
I would get to know their true names too
Maybe they are just 'Fred' and 'Bill',
'John' and 'Jim' and 'Sue'!

Sheila Stead

64

THE KEY TO HAPPINESS

We all want to be happy - I'm sure you'll agree
But to be truly happy we must find the key
First of all we'll define what happiness is
It's inner contentment, joy - we could call it bliss
So how d'you attain this much desired condition?
Please read further on and you'll see my rendition
No, it won't come from money - from accumulating wealth
'Cos working all hours - that may damage your health
But, aren't millionaires happy? Well let them confess
Happiness isn't found in the things you possess
Perhaps pursuing pleasure - then happiness you'll find
No, that's not the way to find true peace of mind
So where does it come from? Yes, what is the key?
Please read further on and my answer you'll see
No, it's not to be found in wealth or in pleasure
But, for it you must search - as for hid treasure
So where do you look? My words don't deride
Shake the dust off your Bible and let it be your guide
Yes, the answer's in here - the key's in this book
So take my advice and do take a look
As true peace of mind only comes when you're knowing
Why you are here and where you are going
So, please do not doubt it but search and you'll see
And prove for yourself that the Bible's the key.

Anne Dalton

INSTANT ANSWER

Tomorrow, a decision; has to be met,
but really it's today;
if you ever need expresso logic,
just clasp your hands and pray.

It's a language that's unspoken.
It's a dove that flies to you,
and somehow, somewhere deep inside,
you'll always find the truth.

Love is all around us.
These words come from you.
Sometimes we slip along the way,
so forgive us if we do.

A journey in life is always tough,
no matter what we see.
It could be going up the stairs,
or coming down to tea.

There's lots and lots of miracles,
that happen every day;
along with our sweet Mother;
we only have to say:

'Jesus, we love you,
Jesus we do,
each day we follow,
so how about you?'

Jan A Krupa

OUR EASTBOURNE HOLIDAY

It rained - we couldn't go to the beach
So we bought some postcards at 10p each
And as the weather didn't improve
We had to keep ourselves on the move
At the mansion they played music nostalgic
Which brought back some of the old magic
Ashley rendered tunes most melodious
In this hotel so commodious

Wednesday we visited Firle Place
A home of leisure and of grace
The heritage of the family gage
Taking us back to another age
Paintings by Tintoretto 1500's
How have they kept so long, we wondered?
Furniture of french design
Going back a long long time
Chests of drawers all inlaid
Very intricately made
Photographs along the wall
The family story telling all
One lady there had married thrice
She certainly knew how to throw the dice!

We went to the house of Anne of Cleves
Wooden beams beneath the eaves
Lo and behold! Ye olde four-poster
Complete with bed-warmer-cum-toaster!
Spindle chairs for adult and child
An assortment of flagons for bitter and mild
Fascinating array of needles for crochet
Surely enough to fill a brochure!

Joyce Hacking

A PRAYER

Father of Light
Father of Love
Be with me tonight
Come down from above

When I'm in despair
Please be thou there
To comfort and guide
No matter where

In summer in winter
In autumn and fall
Be thou with me Father
Whom I love most of all

Autumn and fall repeat the idea of winter,
but there is a play upon the word 'Fall'
which echoes the 'Fall of Man' and our tendency
to fall from grace in daily life

Peter Langford

SEA WITH ELAINE

As I stood on a foreign shore
attempting to judge the distance
between islands by eye,
My blood warmed.
Seduced by smells, strange
and common place, coconut oil
fresh sweat, welcoming.
Your eyes fixed points
under a peerless sky.
As I stood trying to judge
the distance between islands.
Your eyes Mediterranean blues,
corresponded to my reality.
And in your smile, white,
I measured my imagined movements,
and jumped in, strong strokes
across a distance
my eye cannot reach.
Still wearing my socks.

John Stevenson

SPREADING MY WINGS

Way back in sixties, great notions filled my head
I thought I knew it all, and my wings I would spread
My maiden flight landed me, this side of the pond
And I grieved for long months, for my family beyond
I climbed the stone steps, to the bed-sit I found
With my old cardboard case, and the sum of six pound
I looked through the window, to survey the scene
Just back yards and dustbins, the sun never seen
For my mother's front parlour, I thought I would die
My tear ducts dried up, I could no longer cry
Where are the green fields? No sign of the birds
Just a visiting landlord, a man of few words
In dreams I was failing, I could never compete
'Stop whining,' a voice called, 'Stand up on your feet';
'Cause the things that you pine for, you'll find anywhere
And it's seldom a broken heart's beyond repair
Well I stood up, the clung on to every moon beam
And I searched everywhere for the voice in my dream
The years quickly passed, and my confidence grew
Two's the voice of my mother, directing me through
Ah yes! I've been so lucky, fate dealt me a mighty hand
Love, good health, children, the strength to make my stand
Now I've got my own stone steps, they boast an inner glow
My brood won't rush to spread their wings, like me long ago . . .

Maura T Bye

THE LAST WORD

We held him down, though he did not resist
But only winced as iron pierced his wrist,
And cried aloud (and this I swear is true),
'Forgive them, for they know not what they do.'

We hung him up; and soon we heard him say,
'You'll be with me in Paradise this day.'
Can man endure such agony as this
Yet speak assured of everlasting bliss?

To see him suffer priests and rulers came:
Some jeered, while others spat and cursed his name.
But by his words an act of love was done,
'See there your Mother; Mother, see your son.'

Three hours beneath the sun his pain he bore
And then in eerie darkness three hours more.
At last, through tortured anguish came his plea,
'O why have you, my God, forsaken me?'

The rule of law and might I understand,
And pity in a god-forsaken land.
'I thirst.' And so we offered to his lip
Some wine soaked in a sponge for him to sip.

With death comes sweet release, all pain is past:
Was death the refuge sought, and found at last?
But he, as though his work now surely done,
'It's finished,' cried: a battle fought and won!

I gazed then on that pale and bloodied face
But found no clue, no certain sign of grace.
'To you, my Father, I my soul confide,'
And breathing out, he bowed his head and died.

They say a friend betrayed him with a kiss:
Do gods descend to live and die like this?
A Jew! A convict! Yes, you'll think it odd
That I should say, 'This man's the Son of God!'

Nigel Courtman

DOWNY DREAMS

Bare foot along the mossy way
Tinctured by blossoms fragrance
Through warming golden gleams I stray
My leafy path the rays enhance

70

Blushing wild roses here I find
And pause to cup in tender hand
Downy dreams engulf my mind
No reality in this hushed land.

Eric Davies

PAWN IN THE GAME

Life's bounteous cup of eternal hope,
Alas runs dry weeds to choke,
And all beneath this lantern sun,
Are but pawns on this chessboard of life,
Who move until life's game is done,
Nor can we omit one fraction from our fate,
As on this journey we venture forth,
For once engaged we must compete,
Or be cancelled by opponents force,
Nor are there rules to govern our play,
Under this dome of moon and stars,
Or eyes to view each slight of hand,
As piece by piece from the board are barred,
Only the hand who fashioned this game,
And devised in each the will to win,
Can truly judge each move we made,
Was won by false or honest skill.

Ian Towers

EASTER

Imagination! - There I stand,
Surrounded, thronged, on every hand,
By varied crowd, mixed types of clan,
To 'gape' upon this 'sinful man'!
With some, mere curiosity,
Though others mock, 'tis plain to see,
But with the 'Marys,' sad I wait,
To watch this 'Man's' awaited fate!
Yet I can bear 'the sight' no more,
My tears in competition pour,
With his own perspiration flow,
While struggling with his cross to go
Through crucification's agony,
When on the mount of calvary;
While from his 'Crown of Thorns' drips blood,
Which mingles with earth's dust and mud! -
'His sin" I ask, 'What has he done?'
'Oh him, - he claims to be God's son,'
I am informed! - I cannot stay,
To watch his death, - I flee away.
For three whole days I mourn and cry,
Why should God's son be doomed to die
Then rumour spreads! - The cave is bare,
In which they laid him, - *He's not there!*
He rose alive I understand,
But this was just as God had 'planned' -
Redemption for earth's 'fallen' race,
Repentent souls he 'saves by grace'
O praise his name, - now truth I see,
God's son was *Crucified* for *me!*

Marjorie Williams

72

HOW SAD

How sad when the good cannot erase the bad
The depth of passion cannot be measured on the scale,
The loss of beauty and eloquence we once had,
A tree which once stood tall, which had to fall
Where now I sit in a dusty railway carriage on an
                              equally dusty railway track - How sad.
The cows and sheep that roamed the length of this green land,
The birds that soared on high, where have they gone?
No more harvests to glean, - How sad.
The factory chimneys dull the once blue sky,
Our oxygen polluted by the motorcar,
The river running through the meadow, now run dry -
                                          How sad.
Stop before it is too late to save our disappearing land,
And leaves us only with a memory of what
Was our world, now destroyed beyond repair - How sad.

Liz Dicken

CAVERNS OF CONTENTMENT

Moulded mystery of intense desire
Fragrant domain, emotive inner hood,
Seared by nectar in hidden vaults of fire,
Latent heat wherein great gods have stood.
Promote all being, lead us to understand
Penitent forces of transmuted awe;
Knowledge buries uncouthness in the sand,
Ignorance uncovered impinges law.
Let those who thirst partake of beauty's sign;
Let each wave swell to its anointed crest
Then unify, each one in slow decline,
By compulsive zeal, or with impulsive zest.
In caverns of contentment lose all time
The bountiful, the simple, the sublime.

Bernard W Grace

73

APPOINTMENT WITH LOVE

Lead by the spirit, and
In God's appointed time
He will reveal His choice to you
If you make Him the source of what you do, and
Let Him live His life through you.
Drawn by loving kindness
There is an equal bond of love.
For his plan is perfect unity
And originates from above.
Two lives are laid down for each other
That's the way that love should be.
It's something two people will by sharing,
It is constant, true and free.
With particular trust built over the years . . . of
Loyalty, honesty, laughter and tears.
Gratitude for one another, built into the trust
For romance and passion is always a must.
Love is as strong as death, and runs so very deep
You can give, give, give and have some to keep.
With kindred souls, and kindred bodies,
Emotions that coincide . . . This love will be
Tender and caring, and respectful of you,
Protective and patient, and forgiving too . . .
Love senses the pain when you sometimes weep,
Bearing your burdens when the hurt is deep.
For love is of God, it is His redeeming plan
And those whom He hath joined, are kept,
                                        in the palm of his hand.

Heather Henning

74

THE WASTELAND

My heart is a wasteland:
Granular sand,
Where arid rocks sit,
Distorted beggars, craving rain,
Calcified by tears of pain, cried in vain,
Over and over again. It is plain
There is no love left in this burned out pit.
You have stoned it
With a hail of cruel words, stinging to my ears.
They have multiplied over the years,
Spawning a hydra-headed hatred,
Lashing, wildly thrashing: fed
By brooding discontent
And festering resentment.
Love is dead.

Jan Ferrier

ME

Your pleasure's tainted
Now you resent, *Me*.
I sense your shame
I know,
You can't confess, *Me*.
Your mind's in torture
Emotions tear, *Me*.
I feel your heart beat
Now,
Your body shares, *Me*.

I have no voice to speak.
Some say,
I have no rights to life.
Me
I can only trust your faith
And pray.
You'll kill your pride
Not, *Me*.

Lyn Crossley

CELESTIAL BLOSSOMS

It was one of those restless, sleepless nights
As I stood by my bedroom window
Watching as the moon cast its shadows from above
Spreading a silver blanket over the ground below
When floating down from the sky
Came a clusters of snowflakes
Like a host of white butterflies
Carried along by a friendly breeze
Slowly and silently they fell
Soft and light as a whisper
Spoken into the darkness
Set free by celestial lungs
Who know the secrets of the skies
For some their journey is broken
By the naked branches of once blossoming trees
There to lie glistening in the moonlight
Until the morning sun melts their hearts
Flakes cling to the cold window pane
Forming patterns never to be drawn by hand
To be explained only by men in madness
For such beauty in never seen by those who are sane

Margaret Paterson

LIVING DRAMA

During a lifetime,
You play a hundred characters.
You play against and with
Another man's time, another hundred personalities.
Questioning the existence terminates the mystery.
You turn away and begin to venture.
Another time is sought.
During a lifetime,
You inspire a thousand novels.
Anticipation leads you onto each fresh page.
Circumstances draw a thousand new times.
They weave in and out of the tall dark pillars
Separating each locked chapter.
Times are enclosed and forgotten.
During a lifetime.
You star in a million films.
An act of humour supports every scene.
A word of suspense builds hope of every breath.
The film becomes slow-moving, a chiller.
The characters reveal unrecognised faces.
One motion, one sound, one expression;
The music, the curtain.
Every smile is shattered.
Every hope . . . defeated.

Catherine Roberts

CAUGHT AND LOCKED

Freedom in life
Snapped away so fast
One move wrong
Could be your last.

Locked in cells
Far from home
Caged like animals
Left all alone.

Anxiety takes over
Guiltness is out
Freedom is craved
Minds full of doubt.

Convicted, so guilty
Proven; so innocent
Emptiness, relief
A life of Repentence.

Jessica R M Cowley

RELEASE

I screamed aloud my agony,
And it echoed through the night,
Take me from the darkness,
Please lead me to the light.

I tore the rags that clothed me,
Tossed and threw them high
And took a cloud to trim the gown,
I made from sunset sky.

I danced with gay abandon,
Released at last from pain,
I drew a perfect rainbow,
And showered you with rain.

Now I can ride upon the wind,
Or dance upon the sea,
Though you may no longer touch me,
Please do not weep for me.

Elizabeth Whitehead

QUICK SILVER

When you were young you thought your pathway strewn with gold,
The sun-drenched blossoms at your feet a walk of bliss untold.
I also thought the north wind in my hair a lover's note from far
Come to call me softly to the evening star.
Since then dull care has taken unkind brush and drawn-etching
your sighs,
Ambition lost has placed a bitter tic inside your eyes.
I also, when I reached my promised evening star
Found cold and empty tinsel not romance from afar.

Let us then together forget this quick sand
And hand in hand go softly to another wonderland,
Where nought is promised. Do not let us pray
Miss the passing moment before it flies away.
For soon, too late, we will be nothing
Circling around on eternal nothingless wing.

Catherine Nair

I COMMUNICATE

I have said, I like to read
Poems that rhyme, show I need,
That I feel I owe a duty,
To reach you, give you Beauty.

The way you choose to express,
Friendship, love or happiness,
Make it simple, make it true
That those words are meant for you.
Rhyme or rhythm, rough or smooth,
It should comfort, feel it soothe
Poetry will always guide you
Silently, to friends beside you.

Iris Bew

OASIS

I saw you as
an oasis of love
within this desert
named loneliness,
Love's thirst
I believed
you would quench;
your heart the cold
desert night
my pain the cruel
midday sun,
Oasis a man's
desperate mirage.

Cameron Montrose

UNTITLED

It's New Year's Eve
I sit alone
no-one here
to share my home

My family's gone
I am alone
no visits or cares
no-one to phone

They have their lives
no time for me
I sit by the fire
with my memories

They may be gone
they may not care
but in my heart
they are always there.

Sarah E Beston

A.A.

He reaches for the bottle
never been a violent man
years of gin have broken him
from stability to sin.
Finds his only friend and aid
within polished wood and chrome,
the dim lights are fading fast
the next drink will be his last.
Lost the best years of his life
they've been sold for liquid jest
it's too late to turn around
strength for change not to be found.

Swollen eyes and wounded pride
she took flight for the last time
best years of her life denied
sick of all the times he lied.

For the victims of this vice
ignored by the social crowd,
no support for helpless fool
bound to break another rule.

Angela Howard

RESURRECTION

The sun's golden rays caress the earth,
awakening into life again all that has lain
so quiet and still during winter's slumber.
Birds sing sweetly in the trees
heralding the beauty yet to come.
Gaily coloured flowers burst forth
in splendour from the deep dark earth;
I sense their joy and am filled with wonder.

Praise be to God that spring is here at last.
All around me is rejoicing in the
Divine promise of Resurrection and new life.
I also praise God that with the dawning
of Easter Day we too will be raised afresh,
as we receive into our beings once more,
the glorious life-giving spirit of that
Gentle One - Our *Saviour Jesus Christ*.

Briony V Lill

LORD

You gave your life for me Lord
On that first Easter Day.
You gave your life for me Lord
To take my sins away.

You suffered on the cross Lord
To bring me close to you.
You suffered on the cross Lord
What love it took, so true.

They put you in a tomb Lord
And sealed it with a stone.
They put you in a tomb Lord
And left you all alone.

When Mary came to call Lord
On that morning bright and clear.
When Mary came to call Lord
She saw the tomb so bear.

For you had won the victory Lord
And risen to new birth.
For you had won the victory Lord
And brought us heaven on earth.

Josephine Blyth

82

YOUNG MAN FROM JERUSALEM

Greetings, Uncle Barnabas, I'm glad you could be here,
Jerusalem, for Passover, the highlight of our year,
But this time I cannot rejoice, for one I loved is lost,
A Jewish first-born son is slain upon a Roman cross.

We hoped that God had sent him as the one to set us free.
No, he never talked of war, but what other way could be
The means to drive the Romans out, and bring their empire down?
How could he be Messiah if he would not claim the crown?

Well yes, he healed the sick and lame, as will God's chosen one.
Not since the days of ancient seers had deeds like that been done.
He was clearly someone special, but the Christ? I cannot say.
Why should a man so merciful have to die that way?

I wish you had heard his teaching, the wisdom that he tried
To share. More than his wonders, that drew me to his side.
He never claimed 'Thus says the Lord', instead he said 'I say'.
Our leaders called it blasphemy, that's why they made him pay.

I heard that at his trial he answered not a word
To all the trumped-up charges, no matter how absurd.
Like a sheep before its shearers - that's a strange analogy.
Oh! you're thinking of Isaiah . . . Well I suppose . . . Let's see.

Wounded for our wrong doing - it was surely not for his own.
There was no just cause to kill him, ask anyone in the town.
But if he was God's servant, in whose mouth shall be no lies,
Why did he say that the third day from death he would arise?

Excuse me, Uncle Barnabas, I'm heading off to bed.
Another day of sadness, or undreamt of joy, ahead.
Tomorrow I'll be through the gates just before the dawn
To see if it's a normal day, or Resurrection Morn.

Colin Newton

83

EASTER

Easter is not just a story - of a cross and an empty tomb,
of a garden in Gethsemane - or a crucifixion at noon.
Oh no! Much more than this:
It's the showing forth - the blossoming of a stronger force on earth,
proof if you like in action - the reason for Jesus' birth,
bringing its ultimate triumph of love - in glorious certainty.
Of the blessed resurrection - joys of eternity,
which all his followers shall share - because of Calvary,
when his fleeting breath - made a myth of death
and brought freedom for you - and for me.

Morwen Pippen

SUCKER

I fell like the others
when I answered that ad,
and while they strung me along
I was glad that I had.
But the product they promised
just never came,
so I've finally realised
I'm just a pawn in their game.

Lynda Huckell

TO MY BROTHER

It's over for you
You stepped aside and waved us on
You halted that enemy of humanity
Time - before it pushed you deeper
Into the downhill stretch
Breathless and dying towards decay
Left before that shadowy day

And while we weep
Are you watching us somewhere near
Helpless to assuage our indelible pain
Unable to break the chains of grief
That blinds us to the truth?
Do you long to tell us of that glorious light
and whisper softly, I'm all right?

Barbara Samson

EASTER

What! Easter mean to you and me?
Chocolate eggs? Hot cross buns for tea?
A welcome break from work or school?
Making someone feel an April fool?
While gusty winds and sunlit showers
Clear the air and feed the flowers
For some of us it simply means
It's time for Dad to sow his beans
Or take a stroll along the beach
Preferring to hymns - The seagulls screech
As church bells urge the dwindling few
Who yet still care - to fill a pew
Supermarket tills a'ringing
Drown the sound of choirs singing
Is Easter falling out of fashion?
Are we losing the glory of the passion?
The Bible story's just the same
Is it's presentation now to blame
Are solemn sermons - ancient rites
Putting earnest Christian youth to flight
Are we a poor example setting
And the promise of eternal life forgetting
Through the resurrection of the risen Lord
If we but spread his living word?

Is Father time with half worn broom
Sweeping away the mystery of the empty tomb?
Oh! wasted agony and grief,
Oh! waste of love beyond belief
If we betray the saviours trust
And let the Easter message gather dust
'Til Christ returns to earth again
With love and healing for all men.
Let us resolve to play our part
And spread the message of the heart.
To be his eyes, his arms, his feet
And kindle love in all we meet
By our example word and deed
His channel be - where there's a need
And may his grace show us the way
To restore the glory of Easter Day.

John Elias

QUEEN OF THE COTTAGE

She sits in her easy chair by the fire,
While the peasant women do her washing and sewing.
They display their work to her;
She kicks the bone of their backsides,
And sends them to the kitchen to make gingerbread.
They hurry along, wishing they were the roses
On the wallpaper,
Not the queen of the cottage.

The queen cannot venture beyond her door.
She dare not explore the outside world,
For fear of meeting a knight,
Who, after no polite greetings,
Would depose her from the throne,
And carry her smartly to the castle dungeons.

So the queen stays all day in her cottage,
Sending peasants to the shops to buy her food
And other necessities,
She cannot even go into the village -
The knights are patrolling the whole country.

Her own cruelty and cowardice
Have trapped her in this cottage,
Where not even the wallpaper
Can stay rosy forever.

Cheryl May

QUALITY OF CARE

I am quite sure that you don't see
the person who is really me,
with back now bent, must I then prove
that though my limbs are slow to move,
my heart and mind remain the same
And loss of pride still gives me pain?

I was a child who went to school
who learned that teachers made the rule,
that adolescent grown-up Miss
experiencing a boy's first kiss.
Yes, memories are very clear,
not only for the things held dear.

I was a competent young wife
who took on all the stress of life,
a mother nursing children small
or guarding toddlers from a fall.
My sensitivities now show
that what you see, is what you know.

So now I'm asking you to be
not only tolerant of me,
but look beneath these lines of age
and cause no more this inner rage.
Poor *quality of care* does show
if all you see, is all you know.

Grace Leeder-Jackson

THE POET

My poetry reflects mood swings -
in scope - interprets, many things.
Don't ask why - I need to do it?
Probably wouldn't - if I knew it!
And take this opportunity to say,
it sure as heck - ain't for the pay!
Poetry, middling staid, or bland;
lowliest subject - to very grand.
Not just scanning to rhyme good news;
much good verse - just sings the blues!
My critique, may give rise to mere cynicism,
in oblique, and conversely - sheer realism!
But of wit and pen - no-one need worry!
I rarely use real names - at least,
not in a hurry!
And I've often heard this said of bards,
I guess it's just a rumour,
that poets are alleged to having -
quite a sense of humour?

Paul Nicklin

THE LONESOME

John was lost all alone
He had disobeyed his parents
He had left home
Left and fell into misery and pain
No job, no home, no money
Just afraid.
He had no friends to turn too
Nowhere to sleep
One set of clothes
Tattered shoes for his feet
Eating scraps of food from bins
He got cold in the night
And scared once again.
No sense of worth of purpose in life
His days spent surviving
That's all that he knows
He's made it his business
From previous episodes
Where people stole his money
Belongings and his blood
No-one cares about him
So he learnt that he should.

Anita Watts

WORDS OF CONFUSION

Round in circles
go thoughts only of you,
words of confusion
spoken over and over again,
skimming the edges
of hidden emotions,
trying to break through
to get the message to you.

Repeats of a situation
worse than ITV,
in which you plead ignorance
leaving the fool to be me,
a fool that gives you
words of confusion,
too often
too much,
an illusive delusion
still going round the circles,
and round the bend
'til some words of inspiration,
his ego
can mend.

Carl Davies

CHRISTIANITY

The church bells ring, the choirboys sing;
the earth, it sounds so holy,
with feathered bird upon the wing;
a babe is born so lowly.
When Jesus Christ at Christmas-tide,
is to a manger carried;
there with the ox and cows to share,
Joseph to Mary's married.
The church bells ring at Easter-tide,
a cruel cross is shapen;
and so the Christian story's told,
it was all meant to happen.

Peter Buss

90

UNTITLED

O happy, happy Easter Day
when children danced and did their play.
Sun, moon and stars; birds, flowers - all
praised the Lord at this sweet call.
They acted out the Easter story
blessing Jesus, ris'n in glory.
Families, as me, gave voice
singing, 'Rejoice, again I say, rejoice!'
Death's no longer the eternal prison
Alleluia! Christ is risen!

Millie Edwards

TIMOR MORTIS CONTURBAT ME

Be not afraid of life or time
sequence is not with me,
come to the Sea of Galilee
and you shall walk with me.
Then we may tread the mountain stair
which rises to the peak,
breathing the pure, pellucid air
your earthbound soul did seek.
These hours a thousand years may span
or only but a day,
(you shall not know how time began
the angels are at play!).

D E Metcalfe

BECALMED

I have rowed my little boat
Far, far upstream
Where it rocks gently, just afloat.
I sit in it and dream,

Where, shedding gold, the sunshine heats
The water set aglow,
Before my tributary meets
The river down below.

This idyll cannot last, I slack.
The law of life is work.
My little boat must be rowed back
To where the waters fork.

And then which way to go,
Row up or down?
Easy or hard? Impossible to know,
Steering alone.

A voyage rough, or smoothly blest?
I neither know nor care
What place my boat may come to rest,
So God be there.

Joseph O'Shea

40 WONDERFUL YEARS

When I first saw you standing there, and you held my hand
I knew in an instant, that you would understand,
You helped me cope, through the days of bad and good
And you showed your love to me, just like I knew you would.

You never let me down, faithful to the end
And to everyone around you, you were their friend,
You gave them good advice, whenever things went wrong
And many people say to me now, 'You were so strong'.

But now as I see you there, so full of peace
The pain that I saw edged on your face, has now just ceased,
God just came down to help you, and to set you free
And I knew that deep within myself, you had gone from me.

I hold a memory, deep within my heart
A beautiful memory, that must never part,
You meant the world to me, and your love was so true
But all that I have left now, are beautiful dreams of you.

Dreams that you came to me to let me know
That throughout all our lives you really loved me so,
You gave me wonderful memories of such happy days
And all your love came shining through with your unselfish ways.

I see a vision now, of a love so true
I feel a heartache, whenever I think of you,
You told me, 'That you'd wait for me, no matter how long'
Just forty years of memories, that's now just come and gone.

Barbara Holme

SOUL SUNG BLUES
For Debbie, inspired by past memories

If some day I bowed my head in shame,
confessed to you troubled thoughts,
past guilts and sins, could you find
forgiveness in your heart to show pity
and mercy for this helpless sinner?
If then I would in return, fill the
vacuity that sometimes life has to offer us
with love, tenderness, to show you
even a loser can be a winner.
If you leave me now, without you by my side,
I would be nothing.
Alone, in awe of you in fields of dreams,
I would write these words as I
listen to my soulful heart,
inside gently sing.

Charles Murphy

HEALING LIGHT

O diamond bright, white ray supreme
Help me to bring about my dream,
To help those who are in pain
That they may be well again.
For those who are sick in body and mind
Help me to help all of mankind,
O Spirit of the universe
Let man see the light and feel Thy worth.
If man could see the inner light
I feel sure it would help them to do what is right,
For we get out of life what we put in
And we should try more to be free from sin.
Healing white light heal me too
For I feel I know the beauty of you,
May I do absent healing for the sick far away
And those nearer home that I see every day.
Please shine bright on our family
And free from suffering let them be.
My husband Fred, he's the right one for me
We will be together through eternity.
Let us all live happily on this plane for a while
Then one day we will see my mother's sweet smile,
She'll be waiting to greet us with her tender love
Just like all who have gone to the plane up above.
Only when we have done all that is right
One day we will see God's own eternal light.

Marilyn Brierley

I COULD HAVE

I could have been an actress walking across the stage
Bowing to my audience in a bygone age,
Speaking, strutting, acting, so beautiful to see
The stage-door Johnnies waiting to escort only me.

94

I could have been a ballerina floating gracefully
Music swelling round me, the people flock to see
My fans are clapping, I'm in a dream; I've danced for such long
                                                    hours
The ballet is finished; I bow, I smile, accepting bouquets of flowers.

I could have been a model; so slim, so tall, so pure
Wearing clothes made just for me, my future so secure
The world all mine, men at my feet, a picture to be seen
Then it happens, talent scout, I'm on the TV screen.

I have been a housewife, mother, I feel quite proud of this
Cleaning, baking, washing, smiling, it wasn't always bliss
If I had my life over, I know I'd do the same
For destiny is our companion as we walk together down life's lane.

Muriel Rodgers

MONEY-GO-ROUND

Money makes the world go 'round
   that is what they say
      me I agree
         I've had to pay and pay.

Dave Arnold

WE OF ALL SEASONS

Us English are a funny lot
We're not easy to explain,
Grumbling about the weather
Be it cold, or hot, or rain.

We never seem quite satisfied
How the weather is each day,
It's either just too hot
Or winter's on its way.

But when next autumn comes along
With its endless days of rain,
We'll remember our hot summer
Will it ever come back again?

With cold, dark nights, winter chills
Leaves covering the ground,
No more sounds of songbirds
Just cold wind whistling around.

After long, solemn days of winter
We hope for signs of spring,
The peeping out of snowdrops
Or blackbirds on the wing.

Soon, the sun will shine again
Winter clothes we'll put away,
Then once more we'll all complain
Of how hot it is today.

Perhaps one day we'll realise
The weather we can't control,
And maybe we should all thank God
We don't live at the North Pole.

Colin Needham

THE FIRST TIME I JUMPED

She paced slowly into the yard
a thoroughbred that stole my heart
left in a daze, I walked over
and groomed her softly till she shined
then slipping off her rug
I got ready for the ride

As I mounted she bowed her head
then her ears pricked up
finally we were moving as one
together we worked
quickening the pace
what feeling, what pleasure, what fun

Stride after stride we fell
deeper inside,
a bottomless pit of love
she pulled hard down below
as I sat in command
giving jerks on the rein from above

Knowing she had more
I gave her the whip
she replied as she spread her legs wider
faster we went
as I held on tightly
I could feel the heart beating inside her

Approaching the jump
we both opened our eyes
would our tired bodies carry us through?
She started to push
and up we went
O God, what a great thing to do.

Aaron Lee Vallance

PLEASURE

Some pleasures are pure and simple
from spring to winter time;

Like a basket full of kittens,
Fresh washing on a line;

Cottage garden flowers,
Tapestry and lace!

The beauty of a bird on wing,
Soft kiss, upon a face.

A Mother's love that grows and grows,
The softness of a kitten's nose!

A child who's love is sweet and true
Who cares for you - the whole year through.

The beauty of a butterfly,
A scent of rose, when evening's nigh!

A Church, wherein a bell does ring,
Where people congregate to sing.

A tree, before it sheds it's leaves,
A field of corn, it's grain in sheaves!

A granny's face, free from sin;
The gentle soul, that rests within.

A good man to care throughout your life,
Never giving pain or strife!

A book on hand to read at will,
Our cat; accepting hugs!

And - a God who guides you from above,
Who gives you undivided love.

Sheila M Dell

THE CROSS OF THE SERVANT KING

Ah blessed cross of calvary
Where is the servant King?
You held Him for a little while,
But death has lost its sting.

You held Him as he suffered,
You heard Him cry out loud.
You stood tall and very still,
You held the head that bowed.

Ah blessed cross of calvary,
Your story you will tell.
How Jesus Christ King of the Jews,
Died and tasted hell.

But the King of Kings has risen,
He came out from the tomb,
Death couldn't hold the servant King,
He lives to sing his tune.

Ah blessed cross of calvary,
You too will sing your song.
All through the years you will tell your tale,
Of a King who did no wrong.

And as the world gets older,
This story will grow and grow,
Of a cross, a King who shed his blood,
Because he loved us so.

Patricia Griffin

A NOMADIC MIND

I need not be anywhere
So why do I itch?
I please not a master
So why a side stitch?

I'm anxious at nothing
So why does it spin?
My head out in orbit
And why the strange grin?

And I, lay perturbed
Lethargic and spent,
I need not be anywhere
But anxious I went.

T J Sewell

SITTING IN THE PAST

Sitting on a canal-lock gate
With no human-being in sight,
Sitting on a canal-lock gate
But not alone, in my plight.
The feeling one gets is timeless
It could be 150 years ago,
Were times any better then,
Back there in yesteryear's glow?
Then there were narrow boats to see,
Today now there are none,
It is as though a book
Has lost some pages.
That era now has gone
The recession now, it has me
Just sitting - in the past,
Basking in the warm, summer sun
With no thought of winter's blast.
Sitting on a canal-lock gate
Seems the only place for me,
The only place I find inner peace,
Just sketching - some old tree.

Mac

WHO INDEED?

Who always gets me up on time?
Makes sure my face is free from grime?
Who makes my morning cup of tea
and gets my breakfast, just for me?
Who cleans my bike and oils the wheels
and cleans my shoes, both soles and heels?
Who gets me books to feed my mind
and who to me is ne'er unkind?
Who thinks that I am quite a guy
who might have risen very high,
but for the fact I'm rather shy?
Who hates the dog but loves the cat
and never goes without a hat?
Who pays my fare on train or 'bus
and never makes the slightest fuss?
Who is so brilliant, kind and true
and yet so very humble too?
Who can this wondrous person be?
Who do you think, my friend - it's me!

P E Pinniger

... FOR OONAGH

This is my body, the high priest said,
And my blood, as he proffered the wine;
And I trembled in front of the chalice
For I saw the body was mine.
I had thought the price of my passion
Had satisfied sin and had won,
But the bread on the table was broken
With suffering still to be done.
I had known the scourge and the nailing
I had known the rack of the tree;
And I saw them again in the chalice
That the high priest offered to me.

Quentin de la Bedoyere

101

THE PLAN

Lets go back in the mists of time before the world began,
Before God the Father, Son and Spirit had created man.
Watching Jesus with the Father, using such energy and power
To create a world of beauty, from mountain to smallest flower.

But as the time went passing by men preferred darkness to the light
They became so lost, so blinded not perceiving wrong from right,
God watched men whom he'd created living in such misery.
'Through the Prophets I have spoken, why won't they listen to me?'

'There they live in utter darkness, Heaven and Earth so far apart'
God the Father, Son and Spirit watched mankind with broken heart.
My Son, will you leave Heaven Be prepared to live with them?
Save them from their sin and darkness, open the way between God
and men?'

God the Father, Son and Spirit prepared the one salvation plan
That would open the door of Heaven, bringing God to dwell with
man.
Angels raised their swords in homage, watching the King, Gods
only Son.
Leaving Heaven to begin His mission, the plan of God had just
begun.

Angels watch with increasing wonder, as glory and majesty begin to
fall
Upon the Earth as Jesus enters, not by palace but cattle stall.
Understanding so hard to grasp, who but God could conceive such
a plan?
To save His beloved, created people, God in Jesus, Jesus in man.

He came to that which was His own, His own received Him not
Rejected, betrayed, and crucified, we broke the heart of the Living
God.
But God raised Jesus from the dead, the scars on His hands and
feet
Are the battle scars received in love, that made the plan complete.
This compassion, this love and purpose is for all not just a few

102

This plan God prepared so long ago was made for me and you
Accept the love that God holds out, take your place in God's special
plan
Give your heart as you remember the time that God came down to
man.

E Julia Horton

INNOCENT

The cross He carried cried
to the heavens as it was worn
this miscarriage should not be borne
of all the trees in the creation
was it the sole responsible relation
so ingrained in sin in fashion
why should it be held up to scorn?
with touchiness as sharp as thorn
protested its innocence
not the nation's,
so pointed
prickly proclamation crowning
spurred to action
in numbing of its pins and needles
that only partly parried
the blows that harried
the One who carried
the weight of the whole world;
no privileged Pilate
willing perverse - and free
this criminal barbarous insanity of
death defying deity;
obstinately the nails dug in
but driven home deeper still
fleshing out the Roman view to kill
just Jew
on calvary's forsaken hill,

in Sanhedrin gallery
picture permanent stain
to have to hang such a portrait of pain;
nails cut to the quick with reprimand
histrionics in hysterics grand
heresy in history
why should they go down in infamy?
screaming silence of frustration
shrieking molestation in immolation
suffering God, was there no other way?
why on earth this monstrous malice?
could He not be offered
a poisoned chalice?

Desmond O'Donnell

GOD'S BEAUTY

Who but God could e'er create
The beauties of His world?
A lofty snow-capped mountain
Or a wood with mist unfurled?
A country lane embroidered with
Primrose or hoary frost -
The wild tempestuous ocean by wave and weather tossed.

The gentle breeze of summer
With meadow lush and green,
Daisy-clad 'neath skies of blue
And lark song in between!
The gentle buzzing of a bee,
The waft of new-mown hay;
And blackbird's shrill unrivalled song to grace the close of day.

And golden, golden mornings greet all that summer brings -
Dawn choruses and cooing doves - No wonder my heart sings!

As if this beauty weren't suffice
God further stretched His hand -
He painted autumn's glory -
Russet tints across the land!
The leaves that flutter earthward
Are every shade of gold
And should a hint of sadness come
All's wondrous to behold;
For as the leaves come fluttering down
Like poppies - some blood-red,
We catch a glimpse of God's great plan -
New life from what seemed dead!

My poem has come full circle,
Twill soon be spring again
And there'll be resurrection -
Tender buds and swelling grain;
Bulbs and seeds once covered
By winter's steel-cold earth
Will poke their heads up bravely
To herald glad new birth.

No scientist could e'er create
Or understand God's plan
For all was done with naught but love
Ever since the world began!

Sheila Winson

IF ONLY . . .

The old man lies there, listless and bored,
Reflecting on years of hard toil,
To end up like this in a terminal-ward,
Before being laid in the soil.

He retired from work only six months before,
And despite a few pains in the chest,
He hoped for, perhaps just a dozen years more,
To work his allotment with zest.

But now as he knows that his end must be near,
He regrets the life that he wasted.
And wipes from his cheek a solitary tear,
For experience that he never tasted.

He regrets the nights spent in 'The Goat'
The endless pints of beer,
And he never got to build that boat,
Equipped with fishing gear.

And he never got around to exploring the Nile,
Nor scaling any Himalayan heights,
A priest walks in with professional smile;
To comfort his soul with last rites . . .

So what should he do now his coffin's wheeled in?
Should he face his demise with resistance?
Or meekly acknowledge life wasting's a sin, -
Not living, just basic existence.

But now in a flash, the waste seems so clear,
Would the almighty some years reimburse?
But a soft purring sound is all he can hear, -
Someone is starting the hearse . . .

S A Richards

BLANK CANVAS

At school I was told
I was to speak
in a debate
   I was to be the spirit of art

I didn't want to do it

I didn't like speaking in public
why can't art just represent itself
why do people have to speak for it
    I thought

I didn't want to do it

But I did
and stood
alongside
    politiciansteachersathletesetc

Who all wanted to do it

And represented
timidly the spirit
of art.
    The debate was won by a scientist

Because the floor acknowledged her usefulness

I was told
my arguments were not persuasive enough
and that art's representatives had to be persuasive
    'just look at Van Gogh' said the chair

'His paintings make rainbows look whimpish.'

I stood
before him
head bowed
    like a clumsy sunflower

Growing away from a wall.

Jan Noble

AUTUMN LEAVES

Autumn leaves fall fluttering from the tree
Down to the earth to wither and decay
So must man face his certain destiny
To briefly live and then to pass away.

For most men die and leave no trace behind
Much loved in life, in death though soon forgot
They make no mark upon the public mind
Once buried they are simply left to rot.

But every now and then there comes a man
Of destiny upon the stage of life
A man whose name through countless ages can
Inspire a Nation to heroic strife.

Horatius was my Mother's careful choice
My hero from the tender age of five.
I would repeat in shrill and piping voice
The poetry that made him come alive.

In time of peace a hero hides his light
The threat of Armageddon brings him forth.
A quirky fate takes very high delight
In making war the test of mankind's worth.

David Edwards

ANN'S STORY

When I was fifteen I was pretty naïve
But what happened to me I couldn't believe

One day I started to lose my sight
But everyone said 'Oh! You'll be alright'

But they found a growth that should not have been there
To remove it, they'd have to shave my hair

Since I was an embryo, it had grown
But now it was starting to make itself known

In weeks I would have been blind, they said
So the growth was removed from inside my head

But I didn't know what damage it did
. . . did not understand, I was just a kid

108

When they said I'd have problems having a child
I just shrugged it off, almost smiled

As I sat in hospital, I held my Dad's hand
While he told me about the pituitary gland

I got married and settled down like you do
And several years later, I wanted kids too

I knew I'd have to have 'help' to conceive
But just how complex, I could not perceive

I learned to inject myself every day
You get used to it, I'm surprised to say

People say that I'm rather brave
But to the treatment I'm now a slave

Like climbing a mountain, you're nearing the top
You can't turn back, you just can't stop

We'll not give up hope, we will persevere
Who knows, I may have a baby next year

I keep my chin up, because I can see
There are plenty of people much worse off than me

Ann Higgins

SEARCHING

Belong to tomorrow destiny's dream,
See only the past all that has been,
Yourself you cannot find never know,
Words unspoken cannot show,
Forever searching trying to belong,
Never caring what is right or wrong.

Sue Harman

EVIL OR GOOD

She said
'All men are potential rapists'

I said
I don't like rape it is ugly offensive

I continued
But I don't like an anti-man attitude
Is the good man not allowed any gratitude

If I say
All women are potential sluts
Will I start against myself a hate campaign

It's so obvious
In front of our faces
Can she not see
We are all potentials
It's up to each individual
To be
Evil or good.

Hammy

THE TWO STRANGERS

There's a stranger in the playground,
wondering what to do
There's a stranger in the playground,
Knowing that he is new,

All the children round him,
happy as can be,
except for one person
yes, a stranger is he.

Soon he turns around
and what does he see?
it is another stranger, just like he.

110

Slowly they walk together,
Just like the others.
no more strangers,
just two more friends like brothers.

David Owsianka

THE GLOBETROTTER

The ocean stretched before her, clear and blue;
Amanda Jones was bound for palm-lined shores.
She dreamed of sunshine, peace, horizons new
And leisure time away from household chores.
She rode a camel over Egypt's sand,
Explored the old bazaar and pyramids
Entombing ancient Pharaohs of the land,
Then paused to write a postcard to the kids.
She toured the Louvre, climbed the Eiffel Tower
And cruised to Stratford, birthplace of the Bard.
At Buckingham she waited for an hour
To watch the royal Changing of the Guard.
  Amanda, sighing, drained her vintage drink,
    Put down her travel book and scrubbed the sink.

Hazel Spire

FLORENCE

She gazes in the mirror
and sees reflections of her past.
Her bloodshot eyes strain
from years of over use,
years in the cotton,
years of abuse.

She looks behind the dried up skin,
wondering where the years went
and when old age moved in.
It was an unwelcome guest,
not resident at her request.

She found it hard to recognise the face
sadly staring back
from its lonely space,
like a stranger on a train,
it couldn't be hers, it couldn't,
so old, so much pain,
so near to death.
Who was this woman with the
wheezing breath?

Her mind lived still
in hopeless dreams of summer days.
Private dreams, hiding her reality,
her callouses, her aching back,
her life of cruel poverty.

She needs to keep the dreams alive,
without her dreams she'd not survive
the loneliness,
or the fear of needing help
when no one's near.

Carole Wood

FOR GOD SO LOVED

When I kneel down before you,
and think of what you have done.
You so loved the world before you,
that you gave your only begotten son.

To look down upon your son,
nailed upon the tree.
What pain you must have felt,
your son there to see.

What a gift so precious,
what a gift so dear,
You gave what meant the most to you,
so you could draw us near.

To show how much it means to me
Your gift of calvery,
I lay my life before the cross
I give my life to thee.

So as I walk the Gospel Road
till I stand before my Lord your son
My aim in life will always be
not my will Lord, but yours be done.

So as I walk the Gospel Road
till the end of my earthly days
May my heart be ever full of joy
and my mouth be full of praise.

John Jamblyn

MY LIFE IS LIKE A CANDLE

My life is like a candle
That was lit when the Lord entered my life.
It was reserved for me at conception
By a loving husband and wife.

The day arrived that I was born.
The candle was kept close by.
Jesus called out, bring the child to me
And hold the candle high.

Around the font my family stood.
I was blessed and my sin washed away.
Jesus light of all the world
Entered my life that day.

But as life goes on, the candle dims
My sins begin to mount.
I ask God for forgiveness
My prayers will always count.
I know God's love is powerful
Of this there is no doubt.
If I sincerely love him
My candle will never go out.

I look at life around me.
God knows it's hard to bear.
Has everyone gone crazy
Or don't they really care.

Keep your candle burning
Loving your neighbour, should be your quest.
Then God will say, 'come home my child
You have passed the test'.

Sandra Heffernan

RESURRECTION BALLADS

'Where shall I find him
My one lost love?'
Walking in the garden
At the hour of the dove

You will see the gardener
By the flower bed
'Mary' he called her
'Rabboni' she said

Hiding in the closed room
The doors shut fast
'My peace be with you
Your darkness is past'

'I don't believe you
That can't be true
Nothing is different
Unless I see too'

Joy in the closed room
They were not deceived
The Lord came for Thomas
And then he believed

Heads down against the wind
Joined by a third
All coming from the town
'Surely you heard?

He was our great hope
To set all men free'
'Ah slow and foolish ones
Listen to me'

'Stay now and eat with us
Sharing our bread'
He took and broke it
'It was the Lord' they said
Hard graft all night
And nothing to be won
Way across the water
A small flame shone

As the darkness lifted
What should they hear
'Cast on the other side
There's plenty fish there'

Fish on a small fire
He gave them bread
'Do you love me Peter?'
'You know I do' he said

Helen Shackleton

THE LAST DAY OF APRIL

A boy looks over the edge,
and then looks back,
eyes of bewilderment lost in a stinging sea.
He looks down into the dark void which offers nothing,
not even pain,
and then back again.
He holds the words of a prophet in one hand,
lies that had pulled him through the early months
to the last day of April,
and in the other hand he holds the words of hope,
pleading him not to leave.
As time drags on the voices become louder,
harsher with words that cut the skin.
The ghosts which had been vanquished
return to pull him back to the place he vowed never
to see again.
Running out of time,
running out of hope,
he steps into the murky waters,
as the tide rolls in
on the last day of April.

Neil Tuffnell

JESUS FORSAKEN BY GOD

'Twas with a sad and lonely cry
When Jesus hung upon the cross to die.
For God had then forsaken Him
He, Jesus who had known no sin.
That we, when on Jesus do believe
Eternal life we shall receive.
And God our Father would not forsake
Instead through Christ - He then would make
Us free from the penalty of all sin,
By letting Jesus to our hearts - come in.
Right into the heart for which He died
Grace and mercy He supplied.
To all, who by His spirit dares
Walk in faith, believe He cares
About our soul's salvation
Free us all from condemnation.
Go to heaven when this life is past
To reign with Christ - with God at last.
Hallelujah! Praise His name
Jesus - who bare for us, the blame
That we external life might have
And bide for ever in His love.
In Heaven - with Christ for evermore
Because Jesus had fulfilled the law
By shedding His own precious blood - upon the tree
That we from the power of sin shall be
Justified - and set apart
Because Christ dwells within our heart.

Ethel Elizabeth Deeks

EASTER THOUGHTS

Easter time we reflect and see
Eternal life given from thee
God sent his Son he loved us so
A greater gift we will never know
He lived among us and showed the way
Prepared us by example - he'd be gone one day
To fulfil the word his life he gave
Nailed to a cross Jesus did save
Betrayed he was and still did love
Now glorified and worshipped with God above
An unseen presence he will always be
Nurturing our faith till the last day we see

Jacqueline Dunlop

WHEN ALICE CAME TO STAY

When you came to stay, Alice, we had a right nice time
We talked about the old days, when we were in our prime,
Things are not the same, we said, as when once we were kids
Life was quite alright, we said, though we were on the skids,
We didn't have much money, but we had enough to eat
Bread and jam on weekdays, but Sundays were a treat,
We'd have a tin of pineapple and winkles for our tea
And if Mum could find the money, school would take us to the sea.
That was an adventure, playing on the beach
'Miss', would keep an eye on us, to keep within arms reach,
We'd spend a penny on a rock, to take home to our Mum.
She would be that pleased, she'd eat up every crumb
We didn't have a father, he'd passed away, our dad.
But we didn't grumble too much, tried not to feel too bad,
But things are not the same, Alice, is what we always say
It's true, as well, it's not as nice, as things were in our day.

Elsie M Rogers

MY NIGHTMARE AND PRAYER

Thank God! Thank God!
My Dean is alright.
I cannot forget
That terrible night
The awful sound
As he hit the ground
The dread I felt.
As I ran down the stairs
I screamed and screamed
Please God keep him safe
Don't take him from me
I love him so much.
God answered my prayers.
Thank you Lord
My son is now well
And faintly remembers
That night of hell.
But I remember too well
The holiday climax
That ended it all.
The railing was loose
It caused him to fall
As he leaned over to call
His love next door
She could not hear.
So he leaned too far
He hit the ground
It was a terrible thud.
I hate the memory,
Of that horrible sound.

Kathleen Rose

119

THE FILE

Now tell me Sir, What is your name,
Is your memory still the same,
Is your height average or a little more,
And your weight, is it the same as it was before?
What do you eat and like so well,
Your favourite foods, please to me tell.
How many teeth have you in your head,
Can you still count them as you lie in bed?
Are your gums as hard as steel
As you chew the meat of that scrumptious meal?
What do you drink, milk, coffee or tea?
We must know, to fit you in our category.
You may drink whatever you choose
But please go steady on the booze.
To fill these forms takes quite a while.
We must have something to put in the 'file'.

June Barber

GIVING UP SMOKING

We are having a bet
To give up for good the cigarette
But instead we fret.

Nonetheless we won't give up
We nibble this
And we nibble that
One moment an apple
Next a pear
We feel we are going spare . . .
We chew a gum
We go for a run.

Please let us have just one . . .

But no, we really try
And soon the day has gone by.

At night we lay and think of our bet
We have been good
We had no cigarette.

Gisela Cooper

REDUNDANT

To be made redundant is an awful blow
And is suffered by many in life's ebb and flow
To be no longer needed is a hurt you feel
An unseen wound that is so hard to heal
To be superfluous to needs and requirement
A sad day indeed a forced early retirement
What shall I do about my family and home
It's an awful situation and you feel so alone
Bills and commitments and nothing for leisure
An awful grim future, with no pennies for pleasure
Where did we go wrong, for we all did our best
We improved our output, but were sacked like the rest
The bosses asked us to boost our production
It's a crazy world, now there is a market reduction
What can we do in a land ruled by the rich
When profits fall, it is the workers they ditch
Their thoughts are all selfish they just look at the cost
Not at human misery and the livelihoods lost
Where did we go wrong, yes, a good question indeed
If you analyse it all, you will find it was greed.

F Jolly

LIGHT IN THEM EYES

What light in this boys eyes - eyes of innocence, eyes of
our tomorrow into his trust we give him the future.

The big oak tree stands with its branches spread wide.
Today - tomorrow the young now must look after our elderly,
into homes they go as they live longer.

The hawthorn edging hiding the fox looking for its food its first
meal of the day.

Pollution of the world growing people living longer making more
demands, more problems for the young to solve.

The cuckoo's back of the land, it's that time of year again, as it
plants it's own egg in a foster home - nest.

The light in this boy's young eyes is needed now to solve the
problems not by wars, but by good deeds human deeds.

Thatched cottage next to the small canal where boats erode the
banks - wild life forced to move home.

Cup of courage next to the small canal where boats erode the
banks - wild life forced to move home.

Cup of courage must be taken to find answers to feed our
problems of our numbers on this fragile world. Like the oak
tree the fox.

Our youth must be strong to look after our world our family's
our loved ones, the hawthorn keeps harm out not like the banks
eroding away.

W A Hodgson

122

WHY

My grandson spoke to me today
He said, Grandma tell me why,
They shoot the little children
And leave them there to die?

Why are the people fighting
What is this thing called war?
Why can't they all be happy
Like they were before?

Why are they bombing all the houses?
Where will the people live?
Why are the children hungry
When we have food to give?

I knew not how to answer him
Or even how to try.
Just so that I can set him straight
Will some one tell me why?

Dorothy Bassett

FIVE DAYS AND NIGHTS OF HELL

Down the white dusty streets
We trod the road to hell
Under the gaze of the laughing foe
The slaves that war provided
   Lord Jesus Christ
   Son of God
   Have mercy on me

On the iron rail we were borne
As cattle for slaughter
Humanity packed with violence, vile

123

Five days and nights of suffering
That cannot be described
Lest we offend the delicate ear

The lady of the Cross of Red
Raised the cup of water to my lips
Cool, cool water
I blessed that hand that raised the cup
That restored me
My faith in humanity

As in years gone past
The British Soldiers
Blessed the shadow
   of the *'Lady of the Lamp'*
We too blessed the
Shadow of the ladies
   of the Cross of Red

Lord Jesus Christ
Son of God
Bless the ladies
   of the Cross of Red

Claude Austin Lilley

MEMORIES OF YOUTH

And is that lady, dressed in white,
Still frying golden meals,
And is the shop still gleaming white
With its shining formica and steel?

And do they queue outside the hall,
To see the pictures and news,
And walk home past the allotment wall
Still dreaming of the views?

And do young boys wear Sunday best
When going to Sunday School?
Where that day is still a day of rest
And peace the golden rule.

And do the youths walk up and down
One evening a week on parade,
Through the closed and sheltered nearby town
Till the homeward walk they made?

And does the old lady still scrub her step
From morning through 'till dark,
And children play out in dry and wet
Till the whistle blows in the park?

Yes, all these things are happening still
Through each and every day,
I close my eyes and see them
In another world, far, far away.

B D Daniel

A MOVING EXPERIENCE

'We'll sell the house' - a good idea,
So many viewers came in to peer;
We polished and got rid of all the dust,
Fresh flowers for each visit were a must -
If only they had told us it would take over a year!

William F Beck

AURORA

Minuet from Berenice; Watercolour by Mendelsohn

We sometimes whirled a waltz, you in that long
Green dress, and stepped a saraband's calm pace.
We often sang duet, some artless song,
Your clear contralto and my rumbling bass.
We sat and read: each kind of verse we scanned
From burning Blake to Rupert Brooke. How wild
We thought that atoll beach of clean white sand,
The sunlit tumult of its waves! At mild
Amalfi, in that colonnaded pool
We swam together in the evening light;
And under Lakeland fells austere and cool,
We walked by silent meres of still delight.
O slender one, how fine was our romance: serene,
Both puritan and suave at once: supreme!

R G Head

UNTITLED

How dark and murky life can be,
locked in a prison and never free.
Lie in your cell to think of the past,
and long for the days to go very fast.
Get in your cell and do your bird,
they just think we're a bunch of nerds.
Now listen here screw, stop being so formal,
I may be in here but I'm still very normal.
I know I've done wrong 'cause my mind is so hazy,
so give us a chance and I'll prove I'm not crazy.
When I am free I'll be like a sparrow,
to fly along the straight and narrow.
I will never look west or neither the east,
for till the end of my days I want to have peace.

David Zita

126

SLAVE TO LOVE

He took me there in the bathroom,
on the cold, cold floor,
he gave me so much love,
and he punished me for more,
but oh I loved him,
he was always charming,
and so refined,
he had the power to blow my mind,
but oh I loved him.

Living without him,
can't stop thinking about him,
in my world that's so pale and dim,
visions remind me,
my sorrow confines me,
While I struggle with my soul,
his tenderness and his passions,
like waves built up in me,
I run to him now for mercy,
hold me, take me, please,
I'm a slave to love of this I'm sure,
and oh how I love you evermore.

With lust desire,
my mind is on fire,
no water so let it burn,
my mind resisting,
with pain consisting,
exploding hearts,
promising never to part,
lifts the bond that ties,
a slave to love,
and oh I love him till I die.

J Gayle

THE HUMAN MIND

When happy, people celebrate,
When miserable, they speculate,
When romantic, they get intimate,
When angry, then they separate,
When making up, they're passionate,
When arguing, they're obstinate,
When jealous, they manipulate,
When lying, then they fabricate,
When talking, they associate,
When prying, they interrogate,
When shouting, they intimidate,
When telling tales, they aggravate,
When together, then they congregate,
When leaving, they disintegrate,
When admiring, then they emulate,
When ill, then they recuperate,
When standing still, they soon stagnate,
When moving round, then they rotate,
These emotions people generate,
Always seem to variate,
Whether they praise, or humiliate,
Don't ever underestimate,
The Human Mind.

Sarah Maycock

YOUR CASTLE IN THE AIR

Build not your Castle in the Air,
it will only blow away,
build it safely on solid rock, where
you and loved ones
with love and care,
will live in happiness, day
by day.

Make your door of solid oak, place
upon it
a plate of gold,
where upon your friends will knock.
Place a welcome upon the mat, ask
them in
for a friendly 'chat'.

So close together, as friends should
be,
talk about our lovely world, while
you all enjoy
a cup of tea.

George Ponting

HOLY WEEK

Here may we stop, sit, kneel, watch, linger, learn
The mystery that the word made flesh, through loss
Of heavenly splendour, God-equality,
Took servant-form, obedient to the cross
To be raised high, poor suffering son of man,
And yet by foe at last named Son of God,
Triumphant, reigning even on the tree,
Before You rose, according to Your word.

And looking to the triumph, Easter joy,
With You in this Your Passion week we move,
Following Your suffering, how You loved and died
That we might know Your mind, and live, and love,
And feel the joy and pain; of YourLast Supper
Take, and humbly let You wash our feet,
Our hearts, our souls; and be made strong
To watch and pray in vigil bittersweet,

Palms long forgotten, glad Hosannas stilled,
Purple of Passion veiling from our view
Familiar sacred objects - leaving eyes free
To see beyond the visible to You;
To see with Your eyes, let Your mind be ours,
Submit our wills, welcome our Calvary,
And thus surrendered, learn this Holy Week
The awesome secret of *humility*.

Delroy Oberg

DAY'S END

By an open window,
   One balmy summer night
I sat and watched with interest
   A moth's erratic flight.
As flowers gently swayed
   Their perfume filled the air.
Small white drifting clouds I watched
   And peace was everywhere.
Then came a strident note
   A screech owl was nearby.
As I looked he flew around
   So dark against the sky.
For long I quietly sat
   So much to see and hear.
But darkness now much deeper
   The picture not so clear.
Midnight the church clock chimes
   So ends another day.
Once bright lit houses darkened
   At last I turn away.

Vera Hardwidge

EASTER IN ABERMAW

The sound of the Easter bells is lost
in the wind which gusts today.
Rain pelts on the rocks, the gorse, the grass.
Give thanks for the rain. Christ is risen.

Grey upon grey the mountain's layers creep
up to the mists where flocks of sheep
graze in the constant dripping air
crop the grass, and do not care
that Christ is risen.

High on a rock above the town
the church, a granite sepulchre,
tells its secrets, wants to share
the love that shows that Christ is risen.

Sue Warren Richards

THE OTHER CARPENTER

Forgive me Lord
As I drive this nail into your hand.
I am just a poor carpenter
and I have work to do.
Others would strike and not care.
Your pain separate from their hammer.
'Business is business' they would say,
But I must live also.

Forgive me Lord
as I nail your feet to the cross.
My wife is ill
And the medicine she must have.
My chains have bound me.
My needs are earthy
And I do not weep openly.
If I was rich, if I was rich.

Forgive me Lord
For placing this crown upon your head.
I am a coward and your words seem lies.
How can the poor inherit?
It was the poor that fashioned your cross.
And it is I nailing you there
For a living.
Poverty is my sin.

Ron Clarke

BUSHFIRE IN THE BLUE MOUNTAINS

Swirling, fiery, fearsome flame
Bearing down on hill and plain
Without warning sweeping upwards
Swiftly swooping into suburbs,
Without mercy wrecking backyards
Raging, ruthless, uncontrolled
Like a monster, unprovoked.

Where are you, O God of all?
Do you watch as firemen fall?
Can you hear the stricken call?
As the brute makes awful progress
is it you who cause distress?

I am God of all creation
I am God of every nation
I am God of tree and flower
I hold all things in my power.

Yes, I see the fire smoke pall
I see both bird and human fall
and *I* am God of love and care
have you not noticed?
You are *not* left desolate there.

132

I have come:
in generous spirit
buoyant hope
and loving handout.

I will come tomorrow too:
In all who pledge my work to do
you see my hand - my life outpoured.

Now, we see you, living Lord.

M L Mattay

HEART

A wooden heart,
carved in beech.
A love so near,
now out of reach.
TM loves ST
carved in the bark,
gone now,
forever lost in the dark.
Cut and stripped,
and sawn into planks,
an echoing giggle of
frolicking pranks.

TM & ST
now sleep in a tree
for an age,
The rest has gone to make this page.
They signed their name,
with a Swiss Army Knife,
and made a promise,
to last for life.

133

A ring on their finger,
and rings on the tree,
bonded together,
they all agreed.

The spiky fingered roots
are still there beneath,
despite the chainsaw's
chattering teeth.

Peter A Kelland

WHEN IT'S OVER

When it's over
You just carry on as before,
Pick yourself up,
Brush the cobwebs from your hair.

When it's over
You slip into town for a beer.
Coming to terms with the end of a love affair
Doesn't become any easier
With the passing of the years.
In some ways it gets harder.

You worry that you have messed up
Your last chance to make it work,
To make something of a relationship,
To achieve happiness,
Whatever that is.

You consider yourself foolish
For getting into it in the first place.
You consider it wasn't worth
All the stress and heartache it caused.
Most of all you blame yourself
For the hurt and the way it ended.
You're not sure if it was your fault,
But you guess it probably was.

A month later
You lie in bed with your new lover
And wonder if anything has changed.
She has different coloured hair.
In some ways you like it better.
In other ways you wish she was someone different altogether.

Andy Botterill

THE APPOINTMENT

Haste yer'self in lass and dinnae fret,
Am No go'in tae hurt ye, I promise ma pet,
Sit yer'self doon an open wide,
Noo, let's see whit y'ive goat inside.

Ah, there's loads o'plaque o'ne tartar too,
Yer teeth may be guid,
But yer gums are noo,
'Are they bleeding whin brushing or eatin?' I ask
Ae yer breath manky mocket and humming with gas?

We'ell, I'll jist start scalin' and diggin' around,
And clean up this mess, and see if teeth can be found,
Aye, there's cavities, recession and pyorrhea' too
You'll need a few appointments
If a've tae make ye brand new!

Karin Ailsa Robb

135

TREES OF LIFE

Withered roots from within
Snarled crooked extensions push to without
No blood of life runs through these veins
Only anger; hate; envy
Emulates from the tight and twisted mouth.
She wraps a grasping branch around
My child
Presses a crusted and toughened exterior, weathered from
ages of sought confrontations
Against the smooth cheek of innocent youth
And the furrowed surface of herself begins to seep the warmth and
honesty from my little one's skin.
A smile breaks cracking new avenues across her face,
While my child trembles and looks at me, scared during the
transfusion
Hastily I unleash her
Encircle my protective arms around my own
Protecting her from hate.

Erica Donaldson

PC

I have a PC it terrifies me
what if I make a mistake!
Don't worry mum says my brave young son
PCs are a piece of cake.
Just press this and that and that and this
it really is simple to run, then press
that and this and this and that,
you'll find you will soon have some fun.

So I switched on the monster
and pressed that and this
and pressed this and that once again
i gave it my really best shot.
It's easy said I with a thankful sigh
and promptly wiped out the lot.

Joyce Pompei

UNTITLED

The realm above where I belong,
Is a land of hope and love so strong:
I scarce can wait for that bright morn,
When I awake in that new dawn:
Though trials surround me like a cloud,
With faith in Him I walk so proud;
My path at times is long and steep,
But he is always there to keep:

His love for me is here to stay,
It grows so stronger day by day;
I'll journey on for a little while,
And then I'll see his lovely smile:
My life will be forever bliss,
When my Maker tells me I am His;
But while on earth and time draws near,
He is to me forever dear.

G Collier

LOVE

When you're young and in love,
You get a funny feeling,
You know it's true love,
When you hear Cupid calling.

137

Love is something to share,
To show someone you care,
Love is never selfish,
It's something to be cherished.

Love is full of passion,
Such a strong emotion,
It's something to treasure,
Long lasting devotion.

H Philp

TO THE WIMBORNE BOWLERS

There's a corner in the Con club
Where the Wimborne bowlers go,
They go there in the winter
When the green is clothed in snow.

They start about September
When they're fat and strong and tanned,
Determined each to stick it out,
Brave fellows to a man.

There, every day, more mellow
With every pint of ale
They suffer very little
As their bodies get more frail.

They come out in the winter once
To a Presidential meal,
They really make an effort
But we know just how they feel.

Then, when that show is over
And all the wine is gone
They go back to their corner
In the club they call the Con.

You'll never see them any more
Till April's end is near,
When out they stumble, haggard, drawn
And trembling, full of fear.

For then it dawns upon them
That the toll upon their strength,
Has left them realising that
They'll never get the length.

So hark ye all beginners
Before you're too far gone,
Just think what may befall you
In that corner in the Con.

R Forbes-Jones

HOME

A comfortable haven
Of happiness and love
A valuable refuge
That fits you like a glove
Sufficiently simple
Adequately plain
A place to retreat to
Again and again
A welcome
When everything goes wrong
Habitual shelter
To which you belong

V Lingard

TANSY

I have a very dear old friend,
Whose life is coming to it's end,
I had her many years ago,
And I have come to love her so,
Her big brown eyes are far away
Thinking of walks of yesterday
Of good times we have had together
The work and play in any weather.

Her yellow coat and big brown eyes
Her response to orders won many a prize,
Part of my life will go with you
My faithful friend, when we say adieu.

F Laing

PRISON CONTEMPLATION

I sit on my bed and think
of all that I have seen,
barns, fields and butterflies
hot summers that have been.
Sun dried twigs and fallen leaves
for a windy day to stir,
damp chilly mists and golden light
sweet pollen in the air.

I sit on my bed and think
of how my life could be,
when winter comes and snow falls
with hope that I could see.
The pleasure in the different things
and numerous places yet seen,
to see strange countries and changing styles
perhaps visit environments still green.

I sit on my bed and think
of lovers from long ago,
the family who I shall soon see
but friends who will never know.
And still I'll sit on my bed and think
of the many times before,
whilst listening for returning feet
and jingling keys at my cell door.

David Southall

UNTITLED

Inside you my seed grew
both of us stayed so true,
Together we watched your body start to swell
We decided it was time for a wedding bell,
A home we would build for our child
Not enough money to go wild.

How are you my new-born son
To this hospital I have just run,
Looking at you I would say you are a bit blue
Now come on boy you have to pull through,
Your mum says you have to survive the first forty eight hours
I'll pray to the Lord you have the power.

Your mother is in bed feeling sore and sleepy
Not knowing you could die, that would make her weepy,
A few minutes I spent sat beside your mother's bed
I have got a lot of worries in my head,
Home from visiting to a house with no fire
I suppose things are very dire.

I thought I would be pushing a kid round the park
Instead I am sat here in the dark,
I suppose I will get my own tea
Our future I first cannot see,
Young fellow in hospital how long I cannot see
I think I will get on with making my tea

If anything bad happens a neighbour they will ring
Then a child home I will not bring,
First a wife who can only weep
No-one getting much sleep,
I never even expected this
I think I will name him Chris.

Stewart Larkin

MY HEART'S TRUE REST

Like unripe fruit my heart's ways were set;
Hard, jagged and angular as the points
Of a cliff. I was enmeshed in plans
And schemes of my own devising.
When evidence of my identity was required,
I would produce these plans, lift them up
Proudly before heaven and say 'Here I am!'
Yet I lived within a broken frame.
I hurried away my life, not knowing
Where to find my heart's true rest.

142

Though I had forgotten you, you did not
Forget me. Like a horse drawn in
By an invisible bridle, so was the call
Of your Spirit upon my heart. You would
Lead me in the dance of experience and yet
I would not recognise the soft, subtle beat
Which carried your mark. I did not count you
As my friend and so I railed when
Long cherished plans went awry or anger
Was revealed beneath the surface laughter
Of friends. I sensed the fluttering
Of your soft wind upon me and it stirred up
The soreness within. So I drew back
Fearing to know my heart's true rest.

Yet becoming conscious of my sin,
I cleared away a space within for you
To move. And all at once you breathed
Your life into my broken frame, infinitely
Tender and infinitely gentle. My heart
Became quick with the pulse of love.
Sounds and sights I had never noticed,
Shimmering leaves dragged slowly across a path,
Became charged with wonder. I looked
At the chalky lines of an ordinary
Man's face in a queue and beneath them
For the first time saw those eternal questions
Which are the business of us all.
I became alive in your love.
In your light the old bonds and connections
Were broken. I am filled with adoration
Of you, Jesus, true rest of my heart.

Tristram Rae Smith

SUMMER TRAIN JOURNEY

Summer train journeys are such a thrill.
Thro' the window a picture that's never still.
Not for me a paper, puzzle or a book.
I'm content to take it all in, just look and look.
City, town and village scurry by
And clouds make coloured patterns in the sky.
Back gardens filled with blooming flowers,
See old church steeples and modern concrete towers.
Mirror flat-calm of deep, still lake
Into which olive-green willows gently drape.
Field of white-flowered potato, leaves a deep-green hue.
A sweeping expanse of flax, oh so very blue.
Rape-seed in bloom, a startling yellow strong,
Comes into view and then is gone.
Embankment with brambles tangled high.
Sheep and cattle stand and chew as you hurry by.
Woods with trees all in dappled light.
A gaudy cock-pheasant in panicked flight.
In a meadow, to the track so very near,
Unconcerned, graze several deer.
Hawk and owl wait on posts for passing train
To disturb their prey - a crafty game.
Some treat the journey as a waste of time
Thus missing a wealth of sights along the line.

Kelvin Barry

POSTCODE SLIP-UP!

Moving house has a whole new meaning in PO38
No *For Sale* signs go up for this to instigate!
Just a rumbling and a sliding and a crumbling by the sea,
Unless we keep it secret, there'll be no *Sale Agree.*

From Shanklin through to Blackgang, property is all on the move,
'My house is built on solid ground!' is a statement hard to prove!
For the give-away is the postcode in that it tells the fate,
Of the property owner's dilemma - in PO38!

Laura Corti

UNTITLED

Being over fifty, what does it mean today?
Lots of things to look forward to, in every way,
We go to our club on Wednesday, around two
A chat, some bingo, tea and snack for you,
A trip to a theatre, a couple of times a year,
outings, some lovely meals, bring us good cheer.
We look after our members, when some are ill,
We call, when we go shopping, in case, who can tell.
It doesn't take a minute, to call one on the phone
You never know what you might need, living all alone.
When it's a special birthday, we have a lovely spread
I can't wait till I'm eighty, I hope I'm not dead.
We collect 'leftovers', many bargains can be found
Some things we grow out of, it pays to look around.
At times my family collect me, last week Sunday tea,
Next week probably, they'll all descend on me,
Mother's day was special, what a happy crowd,
I quite enjoy my old age, in fact I feel quite proud.

Margaret Williams

RENEWAL

Steam on the windows.
We press fingers on the glass,
Tracing vows of love
In our blended breaths.
We then see our names,
Our hearts, our words
Dissolve, trickle down the pane,
Splash to the floor.
I watch your quiet face,
Your silent lips.
Then I take your hand
And with our twin fingers
Trace again our love.

W G Holloway

SCHOOL HOLIDAYS

By the window my grandson sits
On computer games he tests his wits
An only child, fashion-clad, strong, tall
Holidays abroad, these kids have it all.

Sixty years ago we played in the street
In hand-me-down clothes and plimsolled feet
A broken tile we pushed around
Our stone-scratched hopscotch on the ground
A piece of rope oft spanned the street
We skipped across it on nimble feet
Hide and seek in the park we played
In fields and woods we often strayed
Wild flowers, cones, conkers for us waited
With nature's bounty our wants were sated
Did the sun really shine all day?
Were so many golden hours spent at play?

Now traffic-chocked, the polluted street
Is no place for a child's lone feet
Parks unsafe - everywhere is danger
To freedom my grandson is a stranger.

Dorothy Lane

AS ONCE THEY WORKED THE LAND

As springtime's pale dawn breaks, on a quiet rural farm,
Sun's first warm rays, alight on a scene of peace and calm,
A lone ploughman with his team, materialise from early morning mist,
Gently steadying his horse's reins, tied closely to his wrist.

Two magnificent shires, trudge steadily across an unploughed field,
Bountiful seeds to be carefully sown, a later harvest they will yield,
A quite untouched corner, of Britain's peaceful and tranquil east,
A rich tapestry of country life, upon which our eyes could feast.

A ploughman's respect and affection, for his team is there
                                        plain to see,
His steady hands upon the plough, his crops help feed you and me,
Gentle giants providing working power, as they steadily
                                        pull his plough,
Hungry rooks survey from high above, as they perch
                                        upon thin bough.

A natural history of man, his animals and machines,
Nostalgic memories of yesteryear, awakens dormant dreams,
Brasses glint in the early sunlight, signal direction and his way,
A harmony of man and beast, heralds in this country day.

Seagulls following in rutted wake, exploring each and every furrow,
Rabbits running across green fields, as they scamper
                                        from their burrow,
A pheasant's piercing cry, echoes from a buttercup engulfed
                                        meadow,
Fresh mushrooms spread a carpet over fields, as overnight
                                        they grow.

147

Trudging steadily across the field, now changing to earthly brown,
A shrieking of hungry birds, drowns out all other sound,
A bountiful feast to be had, at this time of want and need,
Once again the ploughman's task, helps nesting birds to feed.

Mechanical tractors have taken over, from our gentle team,
But still those gentle giants, appear from out our dream,
Our world is not always a better place, as time marches
                                                  relentlessly on,
But time cannot erase these nostalgic memories, of a quiet
                                                  and peace now gone.

Jim Wilson

THE PIONEER OF THE STREET

Some people call you a busybody, this will never do,
Coronation Street would be a sad place if it wasn't for you.
Even with your faults, you only do what you think is best,
To turn life to the better, for the benefit of the rest.
This ode is to you Percy, the Pioneer of the Street.

That lovely little cap of yours is always a pleasure to see,
And your charmingly trimmed moustache to a perfect tee.
You're always dressed very smartly and stand out tall.
Boots polished brightly, outshine them all.
This ode is to you Percy, the Pioneer of the Street.

You helped fight for your country, bravely making all that stew,
Now you still fight for justice, doing a great job too.
You held your job as caretaker with the highest will
And now you're head of Neighbourhood Watch, combating
                                                  criminals with much skill.
This ode is to you Percy, the Pioneer of the Street.

148

Housework is no problem, complete to perfection without much
time spent.
And you look after Emily, never forgetting to pay the rent.
You fend of the advances of Phylis, she's not the one for you,
But don't give up looking, as there's many who are single too.
This ode is to you Percy, the Pioneer of the Street.

As you stand in the Rovers Percy, don't ever forget
That you're a fine man, the greatest ever yet.
With the best of British in you, a gracious gent
You would be sorely missed if you ever went.
This ode is for you Percy,
The Pioneer of the Street.

Marion Laycock

LIFE'S PLEASANT CHANGE

I say goodbye to office friends,
Early retirement is the trend.
No more car, it's on the bus,
Summer sun and winter sludge.
Meeting neighbours I never knew
Time to read, knit and sew.
Summer loungers stretched out,
and winter warmth without a doubt.
No rush with housework, just at leisure
Then off to keep-fit or some other pleasure.
Don't wait till life is nearly done
Relax, take it easy and have fun.
You might think you'll never stop work
But early retirement is what you deserve.

Maureen Pettet

MAKING THE TRANSITION WITHOUT TEARS

The time has come, we've reached the age
That youth consider old,
If only they would realise,
But there, they won't be told.

We've never felt so full of life
So active and so daring
We don't care now when people stare
And say, 'What are they wearing.'

There's no-one now to answer to
The future's ours to choose
The children wed, the house is ours
We've nothing now to lose.

We've heard folk say they dread the day
When they reach those later years
But plan ahead, think positive
And don't give way to tears.

The options are unending
With friends and pastures new
It just needs E for effort
But that must come from you.

So why not give it all you've got
Reach out and cross that fence
Where a whole new world is waiting
You know it makes good sense.

So now think back, you've had your share
Of worry stress and tension
Just smile and wait till Thursday comes
Then go and draw your pension.

Pat Sleath

SOLITUDE

As I sit here by my fireside
  In the autumn of my life
I contemplate in solitude
  This philosophy of life.

Years have passed since I began
  The journey on through life's span,
Wars for peace have been in vain
  As countries with mergers plan.
No peace on earth can we attain
  When lives are sacrificed for gain.

Selfish greed still rules the earth
  Where the price of peace cannot be paid,
Mankind must count its worth
  Before another stone is laid,
Or cast like dust into the air.

For man creates the means to destroy
  His fellow creatures and creation,
Greed and wealth are the gods of war,
  They confiscate another's nation
To redeploy, then sacrifice peace for war.

There is only peace in solitude,
  For in nature's world peace will reign
When mankind returns to his own domain
  On earth, or in the universe again.

S V Smy

PROUD TO BE FIFTY SOMETHING

This old bard is past fifty something and in her leisure,
Loves to reminisce and write simply for pleasure.
I am proud to be part of this particular era
With a feeling of satisfaction of that data
When everyone stood together through those traumatic years
Each one doing their bit, who are now old dears.
When our country and folk stood alone
In those crucial days, never hearing a moan,
Instead everyone happy to rally around,
To keep Britain free with their feet firmly on the ground,
Hoping that some good would come out of the bad.
But at that time we probably thought the world had gone
                                        completely mad.
Now we are fifty something circumstances sometimes appear
                                        worse than before,
But looking back perhaps a feeling of being more secure.
That wonderful age of being able to give and take
Remedying the blunders and mistakes before it is too late,
Is something the next over fifties could note in turn
Because whatever era - it is never too late or too old to learn
The beauty of having to work and fight for the important things
                                    in life makes you appreciate,
And to realise not to expect everything to be handed out on a plate.
In those war years which taught us to cope
To look ahead and not to give up hope
Living each day as it came, which was sometimes a mystery,
But I am proud to be part of British history.
Now the salt of the earth evenly ploughing those furrows
For the next generation of fifty something and all our tomorrows.

Nancy Owen

HAPPY RETIREMENT

For many years I earned a crust,
helped stop the firm from going bust,
I spend my time, doing this and that,
and also growing short and fat,
the memories are plentiful,
some good, some bad, but never dull,
I made some friends, upset a few,
and got myself in many a stew,
but on the whole, it's been a good time,
I'll miss it all, well, that's no crime,
all that is left for me to say,
is, thank you all, and have a nice day.

U E Kopf